To Be Like Water

Dear Marcy,

    May your own journey through these movements lead you home to yourself.

Margot

17 September 2021

TO BE LIKE WATER

*Cultivating a Graceful and Fulfilling Life through the
Virtues of Water and Dao Yin Therapeutic Movement*

Margot Rossi

SINGING DRAGON
LONDON AND PHILADELPHIA

First published in Great Britain in 2022 by Singing
Dragon, an imprint of Jessica Kingsley Publishers
An Hachette Company

1

Copyright © Margot Rossi 2022

The right of Margot Rossi to be identified as the Author
of the Work has been asserted by her in accordance with
the Copyright, Designs and Patents Act 1988.

Movement photos by Robin Dreyer.
Illustrations by Finn Rossi.

A CIP catalogue record for this title is available from
the British Library and the Library of Congress

ISBN 978 1 78775 581 9
eISBN 978 1 78775 582 6

Printed and bound in the United States by Integrated Books International

Jessica Kingsley Publishers' policy is to use papers that are natural,
renewable and recyclable products and made from wood grown in
sustainable forests. The logging and manufacturing processes are expected
to conform to the environmental regulations of the country of origin.

Jessica Kingsley Publishers
Carmelite House
50 Victoria Embankment
London EC4Y 0DZ

www.singingdragon.com

To Brenda Harvey—thank you for supporting our community through your wisdom and positivity, dancing by my side, and setting me on a path that nourishes and enriches my life every day.

Contents

Acknowledgments 9

Disclaimer 11

PART 1: A LIFE HISTORY OF WATER

1. Introduction 15

2. Calming the Waters 20

3. The Basic Poses 27

4. The Body and Breath Scan 31

5. 81 and 81 Belly Rub 34

6. Heraclitus and the Yoga Master 36

7. Swimming Snake 43

8. Preparing to Stand 46

9. Be Spontaneous; Be Yourself 48

10. Lizard Runs Across the Water 53

11. Frog Shimmy 56

12. Obstacle Illusion: The Yielding Quality of Water 58

13. Bamboo Twist 61

14. Free Me 64

15. Equine-imity 68

16. Head Roll and Release 73

17. Opening the Doorways to the Earth 77

18. Opening the Windows of Heaven 81

19. The Purity of Water. 85

20. Locust Looks East and West. 91

21. Panning for Gold: Activating the Diaphragm 95

22. Welcome Breath. 98

23. Roll on River 102

24. Locust Looks Ahead 105

25. Returning to the Core 110

26. Unfolding 115

27. Stretch the Bow 118

28. Fire and Water 121

29. The Water Cycle 124

30. Ah-Ma-Ohm 129

31. Agony and Surrender. 132

32. Vortex and Splash 136

33. Sidewinder. 140

34. Reishi and the Hermit 144

35. Circulate and Harmonize Self-Massage 148

PART 2: THE WATERWAYS

36. Introduction to Dao yin Practice 157

37. The Warp and Weft: Basic Steps for Self-Diagnosis 171

38. Case Studies 181

Epilogue: Ouroborus: The Dragon Swallows Its Own Tail 186

Figures 187

Illustrations 207

Yamas and Niyamas of Yoga 211

Further Reading and Research 213

Index. 215

Acknowledgments

I'm aware of how deeply supported I have been throughout the process of writing this book. First and foremost, I want to acknowledge my families, friends, patients, and community. I especially want to thank my husband Michael Stith who championed my vision and encouraged me with every step. My writing coach and dear friend Sue Wasserman was not only able to make sense of and intuit what I wanted to say, but also recognized the moment the words came out just right. Without her, this book would never have been started, or completed. Sue also inspired me through her beautiful photos of water throughout our time working on the book. To Laurencia, Louise, Maria, and Kathy, my deepest gratitude for your faithful friendship, enthusiasm, and seeing and loving me, warts and all. I thank my dream-team colleagues and collaborators—shiatsu practitioner and author Nick Pole and acupuncturist and podcaster Michael Max—for their wise guidance and continued enthusiasm. Thanks also to author Abigail Dewitt for reading my drafts and giving insightful notes on the book and generous encouragement; to photographer Robin Dreyer who kept me smiling and laughing while taking the movement pictures; and finally to Greg Casey, a masterful qigong and acupuncture practitioner, for his valued review and comments on the movement section. I'm thankful to Finn Rossi who courageously debuted their graphic artistry here. I'm grateful to my classmates, students, colleagues, and teachers—it's been a great journey and honor to learn and live this medicine with you. A special nod goes to Nidra Hara who introduced me to and succored me through mindful movement, and Jeffrey Yuen who has modeled living a virtuous life and supported me in mine through private counsel, friendship, his presence, and his teachings. Finally, a special thanks to you, dear reader, for taking time in your precious life to listen and drink in the virtues of water.

Disclaimer

This book is intended to introduce information and practices that have been used in clinical practice and self-care in East Asia for centuries. The information offered is according to the author's best understanding and experience of her teacher's lessons and is to be used by the reader at their own discretion and at their own risk. There are no claims or guarantees for the effectiveness of the exercises. The material contained within this book is not intended to diagnose, treat, cure, or be a substitute for medical supervision. Because of the sophisticated nature of the information presented in this book, it is recommended that the reader consults their physician before following any of the exercises. The information contained in this book is not advice and the method may not be suitable for everyone to follow.

A LIFE HISTORY OF WATER

CHAPTER 1

Introduction

Even before I was conceived, water was destined to influence my life. My parents, who were both raised in a remote area of northern Italy, grew up in direct, conscious relationship to mountain springs that were central to their rural villages. These springs were known for their clarity, purity, and flavor, a memory that remains in the minds of old-timers to this day. They were the hub of the community, a place where people gathered to collect water, wash laundry, water their cows. Because of the integral role that water played in their lives, my parents taught me to have a great respect for it, encouraging me to notice how it flowed and appreciate the beauty of its clarity, and emphasizing the importance of keeping it clean.

It's no surprise that when they emigrated to the United States, my parents found work in a natural environment where water was again a focal point. My father became the caretaker of Hillandale, a large estate in Westchester County, NY. My mom served as a housekeeper, flower arranger, and cook. We lived in a cottage at edge of the grounds. Humble streams meandered through the hardwood landscape, feeding a seven-acre lake. I often walked with the matriarch of the family who owned the estate and was my parents' employer. I affectionately called her "Granny." One of our favorite walks took us to the patch of sandy beach beside the boathouse. From here, Granny's granddaughter (my childhood best friend) and I would paddle out on hot summer days in a rowboat or canoe, accompanied by familiar sounds like the dip and swish of the paddle and the belching bullfrogs. In winter, after my father had pickaxed the ice to confirm it was thick enough to hold our weight, we'd skate and explore the treasures frozen beneath. When suddenly we'd hear a cracking boom, we'd go screaming and stumbling to the shore, grasping at our hearts. There, we'd fall down laughing, remembering it was just the sound of ice expanding and contracting.

When I needed solace, I went to the water. If I wanted to talk to someone without criticism or solutions tossed back at me, there was a favorite stream I found especially soothing. The water was soft and yielding, and much like a pet, compassionate and forgiving.

The way it bubbled and gurgled washed away my noisy thoughts. I've since come to appreciate what the ninth-century CE poet Han Shan wrote, "I'll sleep by the creek and purify my ears."

In summer, I noticed how the water waned, flowing slowly and causing the stream bed to accumulate sediment. Come winter, it was replenished by snow and rain, running cold and crystal clear, once again reclaiming its path. This was my favorite season for visiting. I can still hear its welcoming song.

I eventually left home, but never left the water. I went to Connecticut College, situated on the Thames River, near the Atlantic Ocean. My senior project kept me busy doing field research along the coast. After graduation, I worked as a research field biologist, studying bird communities on Middleton Island, Alaska, and the Farallon Islands off the coast of San Francisco. Then, my dream jobs presented themselves; first, on King George Island, Antarctica, as part of a National Science Foundation research project, and then on the Big Island of Hawaii working for the U.S. Fish and Wildlife Service. This chapter of my life, living near an ocean, culminated in my studies in Chinese medicine in Seattle, Washington, at the Northwest Institute of Acupuncture and Oriental Medicine. In 1994, with my Master's degree in hand, I returned to and practiced in Hawaii for half a year before settling in Western North Carolina. As you might guess, my home and practice are a few hundred feet from one of our state's most pristine rivers.

When I started studying Daoism and discovered its reverence for water, I felt right at home. In essential Daoist texts like the *Dao De Jing* or the *Zhuangzi*, the properties of water serve as a metaphor for how one can live a virtuous and fulfilling life. Water flows effortlessly. It penetrates into spaces where virtually nothing else can go and conforms to the shape in which it's contained. While soft and yielding, it can wear down the hardest materials. Water can adapt to its environment by changing states—solid, liquid, vapor. When it's calm and still, not only can it be used as a level, you can also see into its depths or focus on whatever is being reflected in its mirror-like surface. From the depths of the ocean to the clouds in the sky, its nature is to transform. No matter its form, water nourishes all life on earth.

I began wondering—what might happen if we related these attributes of water to our attention? If your attention, like water, is able to seep into places where nothing else can, what would you discover there? What might your life be like if you could cultivate an attention that is soft and yielding, yet ever-present and flowing? Might you be able to shift certain obstacles in your life?

In thinking of water's ability to change states, imagine yourself acclimating to your environment by changing your state of mind. How might your perspective change? How would that change you? What if, through calm, level attention, you could see the immense depth of yourself in the same way you could see the immense depth of clear, calm water?

Life is constantly changing. The water cycle reflects that. By its nature, water transforms effortlessly from a pool of liquid—evaporating into vapor, condensing into clouds, and falling back to earth as rain. What if we, too, were able to adapt, transforming naturally without resistance as we develop from young to old, recognizing ourselves as a microcosm of the unending cycle of life?

Cultivating our attention so that it is like water takes practice. Ancient cultures offer specific strategies and practices to help us develop and direct our attention in that manner. Much of what I draw on and offer in this book comes from secular mindfulness practices founded in the Buddhist and Daoist traditions, yoga, and classical Chinese medicine.

To Be Like Water takes into consideration that although the body is solid, it changes shape over the course of time. Our form is influenced by our movements, habits, aging, trauma, and even how we think. Our shape changes as we grow, develop, and decline. In this way, we are more fluid than solid. Here is where the movements come into the conversation of being like water. As we explore new patterns of movement with an attitude of curiosity and ease, as we bring attention to and build our awareness of the body, we invite a possibility to change our minds and even our form—our tissues, brain, cells, genes, physiology. This opens a whole new possibility of how being like water can create a more adaptable and relaxed physical and mental-emotional state. Imagine how that would positively influence your health and longevity.

I've composed this book in two parts. The first section is a group of essays about the virtues of being like water, based on my personal experience of seeking to meet and understand myself through movement, mindfulness meditation, and East Asian philosophy. I also draw on my professional experience. For more than 25 years, I've been an Asian medicine practitioner and have taught Chinese medicine, mindfulness, various types of yoga, and East Asian therapeutic movement to acupuncture students, healthcare practitioners, my patients, and the community.

As a way to help you cultivate the qualities of water in your attention, I recommend exercises at the end of each essay. These dao yin therapeutic movements are recorded as I learned and interpreted them through my Chinese medicine and Daoism mentor, Dr. Jeffrey Yuen, an 88th-generation Daoist master of the Jade Purity Yellow Emperor Lao Zi School and a 26th-generation priest of the Complete Reality School, Dragon Gate sect.[1] Dao yin exercises were

---

1   For more information about Dr. Jeffrey Yuen, please go to http://jadepurityfoundation.org/master.html, http://accm.ie/jeffrey-c-yuen, or https://daoisttraditions.edu/our-college/jeffrey-yuen-acupuncture-conferences.

put forward by Imperial Physician Chao Yuanfang in his 7th-century CE seminal text, *Treatise on the Origin and Symptoms of Disease*. I have relied on Jeffrey's instruction and my own experience in practicing, interpreting, and teaching this lying-down form of dao yin. Based on my personal experience of the exercises, I have given names to each practice. According to Jeffrey, Chao Yuanfang encouraged self-empowerment by taking charge of one's health through diet, movement, and self-reflection. Though I describe these exercises—movement, attention, breathing, and reflection—in detailed instruction and photographs, they are merely offered as a starting point. I encourage you to discover what resonates and create your own way of doing the exercises based on self-reflection during and after the practices. Dao yin means to look into yourself, through movement and reflection, and understand who you are. Rather than trying to stick to a set of rules, don't be surprised if you find yourself moving spontaneously, exploring new territory.

The second section of *To Be Like Water* offers an accessible view of classical Chinese medicine theory as it relates to dao yin. Practitioners and patients can appreciate this section for its application. In Chapter 37, I'll walk you through basic steps of diagnosis so you can use your health concern as a foundation for change and growth. Through case studies, you'll see how I use dao yin practice as medicine in my clinic. Putting it all together, you'll be able to select the practices that are best suited to help you learn more about yourself. You may then use the movements and what you discover through self-reflection as a resource to improve your overall wellbeing.

Given my lifelong relationship to water, it feels like my destiny to use it to talk about mindfulness and movement, and the transformations that are possible when we are like water. I invite you to put on your waders and come and explore both the insight and practices with me.

CHAPTER 2

Calming the Waters

Imagine finding yourself kneeling on the floor in a stockroom, hands palm to palm at your chest, tears gliding down your cheeks. It wasn't anything I had planned or expected. I was 22 and all I knew was something extraordinary was happening to me. I felt as if I was a scintillating light filling the space. When I came back into myself, I felt an overwhelming sense of grace and gratitude to a power greater than and beyond myself.

The chances of me giving thanks for my life, not to mention to a so-called higher power, were basically nil. I was fresh out of college, depressed, drug-dependent, and suicidal, my head filled with existential thoughts I believed were true. I lacked faith in a higher power and myself.

This wasn't the first time I found myself having such a mystifying experience. It had also happened the night before, after attending a meditation offered by Sri Chinmoy, a yoga and meditation guru in New York City. At the time, I was living with my parents, working as assistant manager at a high-end kitchenware store in an upscale mall, and saving money for a cross-country adventure with my surfer boyfriend. I remember being terrified by the full-body tingling sensation and intense feeling of elation, gratitude, and humility. It didn't happen during the massive hour-long group meditation but after I had fallen asleep that night. It was so intense, I woke my mom and begged her to explain what was happening to me. Her immediate suspicion was that I had been drugged at the meditation. Perhaps she was right? Admittedly, the meditation scene was so far out of my milieu, I had my doubts, too. However, when it happened the next day at work in the stockroom, it felt like an awakening, one that had nothing to do with something somebody had slipped me without my knowing.

The journey that led me to these fascinating but unsettling experiences began a few months before, after signing up for a weekly yoga class. I was at a crossroads with my depression and confusion about who I was and my place in the world, feeling devoid of a true sense of purpose. At the time, I had a special love for cocaine, LSD, alcohol, hash, uppers, and clubbing. Recognizing that continuing on that path could destroy me, I came up with two options: I could end my life or make a drastic change and embrace the possibility that life was worth living. Weak as it was, the call to make a change got my attention. I started researching options beyond counseling and medication, which had not worked. I stumbled upon an advertisement for yoga classes. The instructor taught from her home, halfway between my work and home. Thinking I had nothing to lose, I took a leap of faith and made the call.

A few days later, I was driving to nearby Stamford, Connecticut, an affluent bedroom community of New York City. I walked through the yoga instructor's pristine garage to the basement door where a sign hung: *Please remove your shoes before entering.* How bizarre, I thought. I had never before been asked to remove my shoes upon entering a house. For a moment, I wanted to turn back, but I was there and I was desperate, so I knocked anyway. The door opened and before me was a woman, around 40 years old, medium build, her long, thick, greying strawberry-blond hair tied up in a neatly combed ponytail. She wore an outfit similar to those I had seen in *National Geographic* articles on India: a white, loose tunic and pants. I was mesmerized by her beauty. Her face, free of makeup, radiated light. Nidra Hara introduced herself and welcomed me in.

A sea-green carpet covered the floor of the small room. Yoga blankets, bolsters, blocks, and a basket of yoga straps lined the wall of the entryway. An altar stood at the far corner of the room, with a black-and-white photo of a bald Indian man, who I later learned was well-known guru Sri Chinmoy, his eyes half closed, looking as if he were in a trance. In front of the photo was a lit candle. Beside it, a raucous stargazer lily in full bloom stood proudly from a simple vase. So foreign was the altar and the image of the man in a trance-like state, had it not been for the familiar flower, which we grew in our garden, I think I would have turned and run.

I found a place on the floor, feeling butterflies in my stomach. After several awkward minutes, a few middle-aged women settled in and we began. By today's standards, the class was basic Hatha yoga. We began by chanting "Ohm" three times followed by eye movements and a range of stretches and postures with Indian names like janusirsasana and bhujangasana. Occasionally, Nidra Hara would chant "Ohm" or chime a bell once we had settled into a posture. At first, the unexpected sound startled me, but then I found it helped me refocus and relax. After each pose, we sat quietly to digest the sensations and note the results of our actions on our emotions, thoughts, and body. Nidra Hara invited us to breathe in while silently saying a word of intent, like compassion, love, forgiveness, or kindness. This was followed by breathing out and silently saying, "I am." Finally, Nidra Hara rang a bell and we chanted "Ohm" once more to end class.

Despite the language and the practice being so unfamiliar, I found myself becoming more curious about what we were doing and more comfortable (while at the same time uncomfortable) with what I was experiencing. Since we'd pay attention to the physical sensations, emotions, and thoughts while in and after each pose, I discovered I had a lot of tension—stuck emotions like grief, anger, and anxiety. Some of that had been brewing for years. My mom, for example, had been diagnosed with breast cancer related to a decade of taking prescribed hormone replacement therapy. Our lives had been turned upside down. As a result of those emotions surfacing in class, I was often overwhelmed, but somehow I knew to stick with practicing. I sensed I had found something precious albeit unexplainable to my Western mind. It seemed to be the help I was looking for. I was not only noticing and accepting what I was experiencing during yoga, I was also starting to apply that attention to my thoughts and emotions about myself and my daily life. As I chipped away at my reality, noticing and accepting, having more compassion, it dawned on me I was learning how to love myself.

Each class came with its own questions and revelations. During one class when we were in a headstand for about five minutes, Nidra Hara invited us to notice if we felt as if we were leaving our body. If so, she instructed us, matter of factly, just to be aware of this phenomenon and bring our attention back into the body, to feel the pressure of the floor at the top of the head and in the arms, stay in position for another breath, and feel the breath moving in and through the body before coming out of the pose. This caught my attention because many times on various highs I had felt as if I was watching myself from a distance, detached from my body and about to float away. Most of the time, it was a great feeling of freedom and relief. I was dissociating and numbing out, disconnecting from the uncomfortable sensations in my body driven by intense emotion. Sometimes, the high led to a panic attack because I lost my way and didn't know how to come back. Here was someone helping me understand that if I were to dissociate, I could check in and notice I was actually safe. All I had to do to get grounded and back into my body was to feel pressure, such as a push against a wall or the feeling of my feet on the ground, and then take another breath, feeling it in my body.

The more I practiced movements and postures with attention, the easier it was to be grounded in my body. Being present to the rhythm of breathing and the sensations I experienced was laying a foundation for knowing and understanding, not just my body and its capabilities, but also myself, my mind, and my energy. I was present with others in a way that was more centered and honest. I could listen to my mom as she talked about her worries, fears, and sorrows, and candidly share with her how I felt without getting drowned in waves of emotion or trying to fantasize a different reality than what was present.

In the past, it hadn't struck me that I didn't need to say everything that came to mind, like sharing my unsolicited opinion or blurting out witty, sarcastic remarks. With this work, I became more comfortable simply listening or being in the silence. I found this enjoyable and rewarding.

Contrary to my prior way of coping with stress and suffering, which primarily involved getting high alone or with friends or strangers, turning attention back to myself and simply allowing what I experienced was revolutionary.

Mindful movement—like yoga, tai chi, qigong, and dao yin— challenge attention through both balance and stamina. To follow direction, shift weight and position, take effective action, and be fully present in a movement requires one's complete attention. Without that attention fully sinking into the action, the posture or movement falls apart, or lacks energy, import, and the possibility of being spiritually transformative.

Giving your attention to what you feel in your body is a gift. It strengthens your ability to notice not only what you feel in your body but also what is happening in your mind. I began discovering how often my mind would wander away from my body and breath into a realm of familiar thoughts and stories, whether past or future, that were judgmental, paranoid, skeptical, fantastic, or cynical. The more aware I became from this practice, imbued with compassion and love, the more I started to question those thoughts about myself and others. Were they really true? What evidence did I have that they were true? Were they true all the time? How did the thought make me feel about myself and others? Was that working for me? Did I want to keep thinking that thought or was there something else I'd rather think about? This inquiry started to loosen the knots that bound me to habitual patterns and kept me from expanding into a life of meaning and purpose.

Over the next months, Nidra Hara supplied me with books and audio recordings on yoga philosophy and Ayurvedic cooking. She invited me to weekly meditations with Sri Chinmoy in New York

City. I spent time in her home as she answered my questions about meditation, vegetarianism, and prayer. I noticed that her life was very intentional. She didn't waste energy ruminating over emotional difficulties or drama. She addressed issues plainly and calmly. Being from a hot-headed, shoot-first-and-ask-questions-later Italian family, this way of communicating and behaving was so foreign to me yet so appealing! Nidra Hara prayed and meditated frequently throughout the day. We'd chant while chopping vegetables. We'd say a prayer for protection after fastening our seat belts in the car and then meditate for a minute before setting off to group meditation; so many actions were steeped in awareness. I began feeling more peaceful. I credited it to this new lifestyle of paying attention that led to me giving thanks for my life in the stockroom.

As I grew more peaceful, my mother became unsettled. Though she'd wrung her hands many a night for years fretting over my mental health, she didn't find my new-found happiness comforting. I was different. She had convinced herself that Nidra Hara was brainwashing me. When I had four wisdom teeth removed and easily breathed my way through the pain without using the prescribed pain medication, she became especially alarmed. Mom begged me to stop going to yoga and stop meditating. I appreciated her looking out for me and wanted her to feel good about what I was doing. Using the "if you can't beat 'em, join 'em" approach, I invited her to come to class. If after practicing yoga she was convinced what I was doing was a detriment to my wellbeing, I'd consider her point of view. Clearly, I was confident her experience in Nidra Hara's class would change her mind.

During our first class together, we sat on opposite sides of the room. She found a place by the door, sporting a pixie cut and wearing the few pieces of comfortable casual attire she owned. I took my place tucked in next to Nidra Hara. Other students, mostly women with long hair and flowing tunics, also settled in. Though her nervous smile and wary glances divulged her discomfort, true to form, Mom remained polite and amicable. When we started chanting

"Ohm," she stared sternly at me as she swept her hand toward the exit, motioning me to leave. I shook my head, "No." Thankfully, she stayed. By the end of class, the tension from fear and worry that had strained her face for so many months melted into a soft glimmering expression. Interestingly enough, Mom became a regular participant in Nidra Hara's classes, while still remaining faithful to her Christian faith. She even became friends with Nidra Hara.

All of this feels like a lifetime ago. It was as if practicing mindful movement and meditation changed my DNA. Regarding my behaviors and thought patterns, I'm simply not the same person I once was.

Before incorporating yoga into my life, my mind was like a fierce wind disrupting tranquil waters. Thanks to a teacher whose presence emanated level calm and a practice that settled my attention and invited it to seep into myself, not only was I able to quell that wind, I was also able eventually to see myself on the surface and into the depth of my mind and spirit.

≈

We'll begin our dao yin journey by tuning in with a body and breath scan. Before we get to that, let's create a foundation with the basic starting poses. After all, as the ancient Daoist master Lao Zi noted, the journey of a thousand miles begins beneath our feet.

Once acquainted with the basic foundational poses, we can move on to the body and breath scan, which is a basic mindfulness practice inviting you to notice what you experience in your body and mind. Tuning in can yield a centered and grounded sense of self. Though you can do a body scan in any of the basic starting poses, we'll return to the supine resting pose for all of our body scans.

After tuning in with the scan, we can go one step further, centering ourselves with a simple belly massage. The 81 and 81 Belly Rub draws our attention to our belly button, which in Chinese medicine represents the Pole Star, the center of our galaxy.

Welcome to the practice!

CHAPTER 3

The Basic Poses

Each exercise begins in one of three starting poses: supine, prone, or side-lying.

SUPINE

Lie on your back on a padded but firm surface with your legs extended, hip-width apart. Place your arms a few inches from the sides of your body, palms up (Figure 1). If your neck is uncomfortable, place a small folded towel or thin pillow under the base of your skull. If you feel discomfort in the low back, place a bolster or pillow behind your knees for support (Figure 2), or fold your hips and knees, standing your feet on the mat (Figure 3).

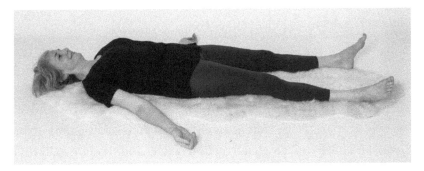

Figure 1

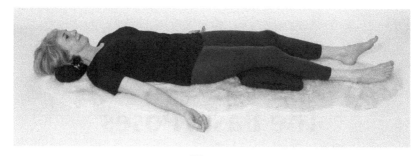

Figure 2

Figure 3

If you can rest comfortably in this position without props, please do so. Otherwise, position and support yourself as needed to feel at ease and without pain. As your body relaxes more with practice, you may find you need less support.

PRONE

Lie face down on a padded but firm surface, with your legs extended, hip-width apart. Place your arms alongside your body, palms up or down, and have your forehead resting on the floor (Figure 4). If this is uncomfortable, fold your elbows and stack your hands, palms down. Rest your forehead on the back of the top hand (Figure 5). Another option is to turn your head to one side and rest your cheek on the back of the hands (Figure 6).

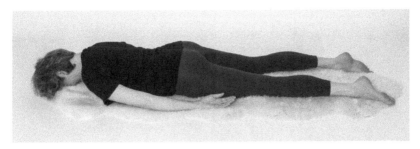

Figure 4

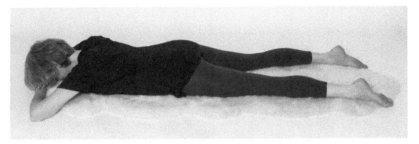

Figure 5

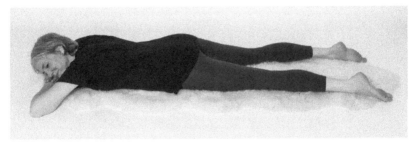

Figure 6

SIDE-LYING

Come to rest on your right side. Tuck your knees level with your belly button. Fold your right arm and place it under your head for support. Your left arm can rest on your left side (Figure 7). If your neck is uncomfortable, support your head by placing a small folded towel or as thin a pillow or cushion as is comfortable beneath your head, and have your right arm resting on the mat in front of your chest (Figure 8).

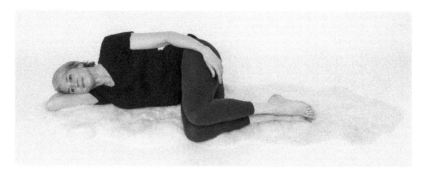

Figure 7

Figure 8

≈ CHAPTER 4 ≈

The Body and Breath Scan

This practice invites your body and breath into your field of awareness. By noticing where your attention is drawn and what you find there, you integrate the mind and body. This invites you deeper into your experience and helps you tap into your innate wisdom, insight, and intuition.

You can do this simple embodiment practice anywhere, anytime, in any position. It calls us to the present moment, a place of peace and possibilities. Welcome home!

1. Please review the instructions for the basic poses. Rest in a comfortable supine pose (Figures 1–3).

2. Move your attention to your feet. Notice how your feet are resting on the ground. Is your weight on the inside, outside, or center of your heels? Are your toes pointing in, out, up toward the sky, or away from you? Notice if one foot feels heavier than the other. Do you notice any sensations in your feet? If you notice a sensation, what single word would you use to describe it? Tight? Tingling? Numb? Sharp? Vibrating? Neutral? Identify the appropriate word and then simply let the sensation be.

3. Slowly move your attention up your legs. Notice how your legs are relating to the ground. Where do they rise away from the ground, where do they touch down? Do your legs feel

heavy or light? Does one leg feel longer, heavier, or wider than the other leg? Note and name any sensations, then let them be.

4. Continue moving your attention to the hips, buttocks, and low back. Notice how these areas relate to the ground. Notice how wide or narrow this area feels. Notice any differences between your left and right sides. Notice and name any sensations and let them be.

5. Move your attention to your middle and upper back, and shoulder blades. Notice how these areas relate to the ground. Note the weight and width of this area, sensations, or any differences between your left and right sides.

6. Continue the scan through your upper body, investigating your shoulders, upper arms, elbows, lower arms, wrists, hands, and fingers.

7. Return your attention to your upper body. Notice the curvature of your neck. Feel the weight of the head and notice if it is tilted to your left or right, or if it rests in a neutral position.

8. Finally, notice how your face feels. Does it feel symmetrical? Tense? Relaxed? Note any sensations and where they are located in relation to your eyes, ears, nose, and mouth.

9. Now that you've completed the body scan, begin observing your natural breathing process. Simply observe how you are breathing without changing it. Please note, there is no right or wrong.

    You might want to notice specific qualities of your breathing. For example, is the breath slow or fast? Shallow or deep? Do you notice any restrictions? If so, where? Are you breathing through your mouth, nose, or a combination of both? Do you tend to hold your breath, either in or out? Notice if you take more time for the in-breath or the out-breath, or if they feel fairly even. It's not necessary to notice all these things, just what you are drawn to.

10. For a moment, place a hand, palm down, over or on the area where you most clearly feel the breath moving—nostrils, chest, ribs, or abdomen. If there is more than one space, place the other hand there. Note the breath's location in your mind. Then, let your hands come to rest alongside your body.

    Ideally, it's recommended to breathe in and out through your nose for these exercises. If you are not feeling well, inhale through your nose and exhale through your mouth. If you are congested and cannot breathe in through your nose, breathe through your mouth. Once the congestion clears, breathe in through the nose.

Now that you have a baseline awareness of body and breath, you are ready to begin the movements. Each movement begins and ends with this scan, helping you become aware of the subtle or obvious changes resulting from the movements. These pauses for reflection and discovery are important and can be pleasurable—so much so, you may want to savor them.

CHAPTER 5

81 and 81 Belly Rub

The 81 and 81 Belly Rub is an abdominal massage that gets us in touch with our center. In Chinese medicine and philosophy, the umbilicus is like the Pole Star or the center of our personal universe. This exercise concentrates our energy around our center and can yield a profound sense of grounding. Be sure to finish with a body and breath scan so you can notice the effects of massaging your belly. This practice can also benefit the intestines: the clockwise massage supports bowel movement while the counterclockwise massage can be useful to curtail excess bowel movement.

1. Rest in a supine pose (Figures 1–3).

2. Please begin with a body and breath scan.

3. Interlace your fingers and place your palms on your abdomen, just below the belly button (Figure 9).

4. Massage your belly by sliding your hands in a circular, clockwise motion around the belly button 81 times. (For clockwise, from the starting position, slide your hands toward your right hip, then up toward your right ribs, across toward your left ribs, and down toward your left hip.) Keep the hands on the soft part of the belly as you move.

5. Notice the size of the circle and the speed with which you

move. Experiment with big and small circles, as well as moving at a fast or slow pace. Discover the size and pace you prefer.

6. Notice any sensations in your shoulders, arms, chest, upper back, belly, and anywhere else that calls your attention.

7. Do any thoughts or emotions arise? If so, just note them and let them be.

8. After you finish 81 revolutions clockwise, do the same massage in the opposite direction, 81 times.

9. Notice any sensations in your shoulders, arms, chest, upper back, belly, and anywhere else that calls your attention as you go in this counterclockwise direction.

10. Notice if your face feels flushed. Do any areas of your body feel cool or hot?

11. When complete, rest with your arms by your sides and do another body and breath scan.

Figure 9

CHAPTER 6

Heraclitus and the Yoga Master

When I begin a movement class or workshop, I ask if anyone is new to the movement practice. I invite participants to share if there's any area of the body or particular asana or movement they'd like to explore. Some folks chime in. It is not uncommon to hear moans or sighs when there's a request for hip opening or balance poses. I check in to see if anyone has a concern or apprehension about what they might experience. There are always at least a couple of hands that are raised. While I would expect concern from people new to the practice, it's often the seasoned students who raise their hands. Thanks to my personal and professional experience in yoga, ballet, and bellydance, I know movement can bring up fear and insecurity.

Getting into sticky places like tight hips, not feeling confident about what we are doing, or feeling uncertain about what to expect can elicit thoughts and images, and concerns about measuring up or keeping up. These things can also trigger traumatic memories, or emotions like fear, grief, or anger. Conversely, knowing gives us a false sense of security and control. It can stoke our self-pride, which can contribute to a lot of ego energy in the room. These by-products of not knowing and knowing bump up against our limitations and capabilities, leading us to feel stuck, frustrated, fearful, sad, inferior, superior, or proud. I was reminded of my own personal experience of this recently when I was trying to reconnect with one of my most beloved mindful movement instructors.

Treya nurtured and deepened my understanding of yoga for many formative years while I was training in acupuncture and Asian medicine in Seattle. Strangely, after 2010, there was no updated information on the web about her thriving movement studio, yoga retreats, and therapeutic massage practice. Eventually, I found her and discovered she had been diagnosed with amyotrophic lateral sclerosis (ALS). I wondered how one so brilliant, passionate, and perceptive about movement faces a neurological disease that involves progressive weakness, ultimately limiting one's ability to move, speak, eat, and breathe.

What I cherish most about Treya's teachings echoes what the philosopher Heraclitus said: "No man ever steps in the same river twice, for it's not the same river and he's not the same man." No matter how proficient her students got with yoga, she encouraged us to continue participating in beginner classes. Reflecting on what I learned about the gift of beginner's mind, especially when facing challenges, I wondered how she was applying what she taught so well.

I met Treya at a movement studio in the Capitol Hill area of Seattle. My former husband discovered her Feldenkrais classes when seeking help for his low back and knee pain. He encouraged me to accompany him to one of her yoga classes. Before we moved to Seattle for me to go to graduate school for acupuncture, I had a rich yoga practice. When we first moved there, I found a group of Sri Chinmoy's disciples nearby and continued my chanting, meditation, and Hatha yoga practice with them. When I arrived at Treya's yoga studio, I didn't check my ego at the door. I was certain I knew what yoga was—not the fluff most people were practicing, but the "real" guru-informed yoga. And I was good at it.

Though the first bits of movement, breathing, and focus were familiar, Treya sequenced them quite differently from a typical Hatha yoga class. The movements were slowed way down. She kept inviting us to notice specific parts of our anatomy—where the weight was, what sensations we were aware of, what responses and tendencies our bodies had as we moved this way or that. At some point, we moved from the tumbling mats to an area where ballet barres were secured to the wall. Treya instructed each of us to place the yoga strap that was hooked around the barre over and around our hips and step our heels back to the wall. She then invited us to bend forward from our hips and hang, supported by the strap and the barre. I remember feeling a twinge of panic. I had never used this strap and barre prop in any other class. I didn't know what to expect, how it was going to feel, or if I was going to do it right. I was just going to have to go with the flow with a group of people I didn't know, which put me even further out of my comfort zone.

Going into the inversion, feeling the pull back from the strap on my hips, I surrendered my torso forward and down, like a waterfall. Placing my palms lightly onto the floor, I stepped my heels back to the wall and took refuge in the familiarity of downward dog pose. Treya invited us to relax and allow the support of the strap to help us let go, let the spine yield to gravity, lengthen, and soften. She recommended we subtly wave the spine up and down, and side to side, as if we were floating like seaweed in a gently swaying current.

The feeling of support, release, and tenderness to my spine over-whelmed me. I felt a rush of energy to my head, feeling as if I was going to pass out. I had no choice but to carefully crumple myself from the strap onto the floor, sitting with my hips folded onto my knees and forehead resting on the floor.

Treya came to my side and gently placed her palm on my back between my shoulder blades, before looking me in the eyes. She smiled a beautiful, sweet smile. Quietly and compassionately, she chuckled and asked what I was feeling. She invited me to simply acknowledge, welcome, and experience the movement of energy that brought me to my knees. She encouraged me to stay there, breathing with awareness, until I felt ready to continue with the rest of the class.

What made me realize I had again found a great teacher was not only how easily she helped me regain my footing, but also that she did it in a way that helped me not judge myself. The situation made me painfully aware that my ego and left brain had overridden my innocence, causing me to think I knew all there was to know about yoga.

It's understandable to think that we know how to "do" something or what to expect from it just because we've done it a hundred times. Over the next three years, I realized I had only begun to scratch the surface with my previous yoga experience. Treya's classes continually challenged me: first, by virtue of the advanced postures; second, and more importantly, she invited us to approach the practice with a sense of curiosity, innocence, and detachment from the outcome. She welcomed the body—its wisdom and responses—into the conversation.

Treya's chuckle was a welcome friend when the asanas challenged me. One of the greatest gifts of developing a beginner's mind was learning how to laugh at myself, to loosen my grip on expectations, and not to take yoga or myself so seriously.

That beginner's mind was fortified when Treya's spiritual mentor Jean Klein came to Seattle to teach a special yoga workshop at her studio.

Jean was a musicologist, medical doctor, and spiritual teacher of yoga and Advaita Vedanta,[1] India's philosophy and meditation tradition of self-realization and non-dualism. He was unlike anyone I had ever met. It were as if he knew a secret about reality. On the surface, Jean was a frail-looking man in his 80s, with thinning, wispy white hair. He spoke English with a German/French accent. I remember him wearing relaxed and loose ivory-colored linen. He sat on a makeshift dais, which allowed him to be seen by the large

---

1 To learn more about Vedanta, I recommend *Vedantic Meditation: Lighting the Flame of Awareness* by David Frawley or one of Jean's insightful books—my favorite is *The Ease of Being.*

crowd that had gathered. Though soft-spoken, he had an intense presence, both daunting and magnetic.

Unlike that first yoga class with Treya, not only was I at ease with having no idea what was going to happen with this extraordinary being, I was also excited. We started with slow, simple, rhythmic movements. Jean's instruction took us from moving as individuals into moving as a collective, like individual drops of water that become a wave. He asked us to close our eyes, to listen carefully from our center. "Breathe," he offered. We felt the weight of the body as we exhaled, its lightness as we inhaled.

There was silence between invitations to move in a certain direction, which gave us pause to notice what we were experiencing. Jean guided us to turn our attention and open to the neutral space between that weight and lightness, and then to our awareness of that space. The feeling of being that empty place of awareness was euphoric. I felt as if I were a wide-open sky, totally free, open to all possibilities.

When I look back on that experience now, I am reminded of a lesson I share with my acupuncture students as they are learning how to hold a needle and insert it painlessly. The story comes from a Daoist master, Zhuangzi. It goes like this: Prince Wen Hui had a cook. Over 19 years, the cook's knife never needed sharpening. When the prince asked the cook why his knife never dulled, the cook revealed that his blade never touched substance, just the space between flesh and bone. Cook exerted no effort, yet the meat would fall to the ground by his feet with a thud.

Under Jean's guidance, just as effortlessly as the cook wielded his knife, we found ourselves upside down, balanced preposterously, silent and aware. This was not the result of ample practice, effort, strength, flexibility, or knowing how to do what we were doing. On the contrary, these gravity-defying postures happened somewhere in the still, silent pauses between inhalation and exhalation, between moving right and left, up and down. Jean was able to lead us into a space of neutral mind, simply through his presence and his invitation to turn our attention to our awareness. Of course, the moment my mind engaged to investigate myself, I became fearful or excited about what my body was doing, and I toppled over. Unlike before when the surprise of the experience triggered panic as I spilled from the strap onto the floor, now I could greet myself with laughter and surrender. It was all so easy and delightful.

Had I been judging my teacher, myself, or my fellow students (that happens, too), or thinking I knew how to do yoga and what it was about, the experience of we-ness, of no-me-ness, of just being, would not have happened.

When I think about beginner's mind in relation to water, I'm drawn to the way water flows seemingly without judgment or anticipation, over and around obstacles, moving even into deep, dark, sullied places. When our attention is like flowing water, unfettered by knowing, we are free to penetrate both the moment and awareness itself. We can explore the terrain of our experience with innocence, curiosity, and wonder. I appreciate world-renowned martial artist Bruce Lee's advice (1971): "Empty your mind, be formless, shapeless like water. Be water, my friend."

Treya would end yoga class with a restorative pose like savasana (corpse pose) followed by a seated meditation. Sometimes, she would invite us to notice and direct the energy moving in our body, offering a visualization or particular way of concentrating or breathing. At the end, she'd invite us to just let go of the doing. "Nothing to do. Nowhere to go. Just be," I can still hear her say.

I've recently discovered, through renewed contact, that Treya is approaching her experience of ALS in the spirit of beginner's mind. She is doing what she can medically to slow the disease process while living life to its fullest with plenty of inner exploration, presence, grace, wisdom, acceptance, and generosity.

In my own life, I am intentional about being vigilant to embrace beginner's mind. It's essential. Without it, I would spend too much time and energy visioning and planning, living in the future, anticipating. Were I to have an unpleasant exchange or regret something

I did or said, I'd linger in the past. When I studied with a teacher, I'd notice my tendency to critique their teaching style. I'm aware of my desire to keep the good stuff and change, improve, or fix what I don't like. Through this awareness, the knot of knowing, of controlling, is loosened and I am more able to experience with acceptance and compassion what is here and now. (In fact, if you could read my thought bubbles, you'd frequently see one that says, "This is what is present for me right now. I can welcome it with a few breaths.")

When I embody beginner's mind with patients in my Asian medicine practice, the welcoming of what is here in the moment opens a space for them to relate to their experience, which is often fraught with anxiety, grief, worry, or fear, with a sense of curiosity.

In this safe container of presence and acceptance, they can explore the internal terrain of their experience with freedom and innocence. What they discover is so rich, far beyond what a diagnosis and treatment plan could offer. Beginner's mind allows us to see the potential resource for healing and growth that lives within the difficulty.

When I think of movements that offer the opportunity to let go of the knowing mind and be receptive to what is here now, Swimming Snake and Preparing to Stand come to mind.

CHAPTER 7

Swimming Snake

This twist activates and releases the Shao Yang system (see Chapter 37). In step 4, the second arm position engages the shoulder blades and upper spine, thereby also engaging the Tai Yang system.

Even though this exercise may be familiar from childhood, I invite you to experience it with a beginner's mind, free from past experience. If you pay attention in this fresh way, you may discover a surprising sense of freedom. It can be quite delightful.

1. Begin in a comfortable supine position (Figures 1–3).

2. Please do a body and breath scan.

3. Bend your hips and knees to stand your feet on the mat (Figure 3). Press your ankles together and keep them together throughout the exercise as if they were bound. While remaining relaxed, do your best not to let them slip past each other. If your legs feel strained, experiment by placing your heels closer to or further away from your buttocks.

4. Next, choose whether you'd like your arms open to the sides in a T-shape, level with your shoulders, palms up (Figure 10), or resting on the floor overhead as straight and relaxed as possible, palms up (Figure 11).

5. Inhale and notice how you feel in this starting position, especially in your arms, shoulders, upper back, and chest.

6. Exhale and twist, allowing your knees to fall to one side. It's important to go only as far as is comfortable. Do your best to keep your ankles together (Figure 12).

7. Inhale, returning to the starting position with the feet standing and knees pointing toward the sky. Notice the weight of your legs as you return to the starting position.

8. Exhale and let your knees fall as you twist to the other side.

9. Set a rhythm as you continue twisting from side to side, synchronizing the movement with your breathing. You decide the speed that's best for you. I encourage you to try both fast and slow to discover which resonates most.

10. Notice if your body begins sliding down your mat as if you're a snake swimming along the surface of a river.

11. If your arms are overhead, notice if you feel an opening in your chest, armpits, ribs, shoulder blades, neck, and arms.

12. "Swim" for a minute and notice if there is any tension or holding. If so, where do you feel it? Is one side more tense than the other? Simply pay attention and let that information sink in.

13. Rest with your legs extended on the mat, with your arms alongside your body, palms up. Repeat the body and breath scan. What do you notice now? Has anything changed from the first body scan? For example, does one side feel heavy or longer? If so, is that your dominant or non-dominant side? What, if any, sensations do you feel? Simply be curious.

Figure 10

Figure 11

Figure 12

CHAPTER 8

Preparing to Stand

I remember watching my baby son lift his heels while pressing down on his toes as he lay in his crib playing with a toy. When he started pulling himself up to standing, he initially stood on his toes. Bending the knees, standing the feet, and pressing the toes down to lift the heels can strengthen our ability to stand up from resting seated position.

1. Begin in a supine pose with your feet standing flat on the floor (Figure 3) and do a body and breath scan.

2. Notice the pressure in the soles of your feet as they contact the ground.

3. Experiment with shifting your feet closer to and further away from your buttocks to find the position that puts the most evenly distributed weight in the soles of your feet. Maintain that distance.

4. Experiment with shifting your feet closer to and further apart from each other to find the distance that creates the most even distribution of weight in the soles of the feet. Relax into this "sweet spot."

5. Inhale and lift your heels off the ground, pressing the balls of your feet as well as your toes into the ground (Figure 13).

6. Exhale and release your heels back to the ground.

7. Repeat for a total of nine times, inhaling to lift your heels and exhaling to rest.

8. Rest with your knees bent and notice if any part of your back feels heavier and in clearer contact with the ground. What other sensations, if any, do you notice?

Figure 13

CHAPTER 9

Be Spontaneous;
Be Yourself

Three years after starting my private practice, I felt ready to deepen my understanding of Chinese medicine. This led my former clinic partner and best friend Dave Lerner and me to create a three-month internship in herbal medicine and qigong at China's Chengdu University of Traditional Chinese Medicine, where a few of our teachers had trained.

When we arrived in Chengdu, we were surprised by the chaos we encountered going to and from our teachers' clinics. It wasn't the amount of traffic that was the issue. I was comfortable driving in such heavily trafficked cities as New York, Seattle, or Milan, but busy Chengdu, with a population of 10 million, was a beast of its own. Drivers sometimes used whichever side of the road was least occupied, and frequently veered into oncoming traffic as they maneuvered around throngs of pedestrians or whining mopeds, some exquisitely draped with a flayed pig or goat, some carrying a side-sitting third passenger.

Every day, I rode my bicycle to my teacher's clinic, surrounded by a mass of cyclists. Sometimes, our handlebars were close enough to touch. Riding among them required me to respond to a barrage of sensory information: the chiming of handlebar bells as people communicated their proximity or their change of position, riders shifting speed or direction, and the unpredictable movement of cars and pedestrians. At first, I tried to pay attention to all these cues and variables, which demanded great focus and caused me great anxiety. That anxiety initially contributed to my crashing into others. I trusted that the more I rode, the easier it would become. As it turned out, I discovered the secret to riding successfully in the pack through an unusual qigong training.

When we arrived in Chengdu, we knew the university would provide qigong lessons. What I didn't know was that serendipity would manifest an additional qigong training, the impact of which was transformational. It arrived in the form of two women whom Dave and I met at the university's guest house. They were on their way to their qigong master in the southeastern part of the city and invited us to join them.

After a wild taxi ride through Chengdu's labyrinth, we arrived at an alley open only to pedestrians and cyclists. It was lined on both sides with cinder-block garages and people squatting or standing on the sidewalk, selling and buying a variety of wares. We made our way through the noisy crowd to a garage near the end of the alley.

A few people were inside, moving slowly in silence. We were greeted in English by a stocky German fellow named Martin. He was the apprentice to the qigong master, who wasn't there that day. Martin welcomed us and instructed us to stand facing a wall, which was painted top to bottom with a figure of Guan Yin, the bodhisattva of compassion, mercy, and kindness.

He explained that the genderless saint holds in their outstretched hand an ampule containing an elixir to heal all suffering. He then directed us to imagine the elixir pouring from the tipped ampule into the top of our heads. Martin invited us to breathe mindfully, feeling or imagining the elixir moving through our bodies, from head to toe, like streams of energy. As the energy moved, we were to notice any sensations and let our intuition guide our movements.

Although there was no music, the woman next to me was alternately writhing, shaking, and swaying, all the while looking grounded and peaceful. Occasionally, she'd blurt out some sound, grunt, or groan. Though I understood Martin's instructions intellectually, I wasn't able to embody them. Feeling awkward, I simply stood there looking at Guan Yin, moving my arms a bit, shifting my weight from side to side, just to do something. I left feeling more tense than when I had arrived.

The following week, with the master present, Martin let us know this movement practice was a form of spontaneous qigong. There were deliberately no fixed movements or obligatory postures, nor was there a goal. He invited us to be like water, which flows according to its nature, responding effortlessly and spontaneously to whatever it encounters. This type of uninhibited movement allows energy to move and blockages to clear without force or intention.

Once again, I stood in front of Guan Yin and imagined the elixir pouring into my body. I still couldn't embrace the practice and hoped the qigong master would notice my discomfort and either show me what to do or at least give me a hint.

Finally, the master came over. He picked up my wrist and began swinging my arm forward and back, causing me to lose my balance. Next, he pressed on my feet and heels and held them down. I felt my spine elongate. Indicating I should keep that feeling of weight in my feet, he asked me to notice what I felt elsewhere in my body. Where was my energy flowing? Where was it stuck? After indicating with his own movement how I could let myself investigate by twisting and swaying, he left me and checked on Dave. I did my best to relax, feel my feet grounding, notice the energy moving through me with each breath, and allow myself to move, all while looking at Guan Yin. Without the refuge of prescribed postures, choreography, or moment-to-moment guidance as I had been accustomed to in my years of yoga, I simply couldn't relax.

Eventually, the master returned. He told me my energy was locked in my armpits, blocking circulation from my chest into my head, arms, and hands. Standing behind me, he slid his fingers deep into my armpits and, with firm pressure, repeatedly strummed what felt like a tight bundle of strings deep inside. Electrical sensations shot through my upper body. Noting my jolts with each shocking stroke, and then my immediate relaxation, he smiled and nodded his approval. He pushed me from side to side to test my balance and grounding. The broad smile on his face indicated he was pleased with what had changed. What amazed me was how I felt in my body and mind. With that tension released, my mind relaxed, allowing me to be aware of the energy flowing through my body.

As I looked at Guan Yin, it was easier to imagine the elixir pouring from the ampule into the top of my head and feel it working its way downward into my torso, limbs, hands, and feet. It felt like a streaming, tingly, shimmering light. I was no longer concerned about how I looked, what I was supposed to be doing, or what the experience was designed to teach. Instead, I was looking within myself rather than following any outside influence. As I closed my eyes to continue focusing my mind inward, I found myself beginning to sway, as if moved by a current.

The capacity to intentionally tap into the mind-body current reminded me of moments in yoga practice. Since the environment in Chengdu was so new and foreign, tapping into my body and beginner's mind was, at first, a challenge. Eventually, these qigong sessions began informing my daily experiences in the city. For example, by tapping into the mind-body current, I was able to navigate Chengdu traffic with greater ease. I discovered, in fact, an exquisite orderliness to the flow that initially seemed so chaotic. The realization I could absorb the detailed information about my environment and how others were maneuvering without strain or worry was freeing.

From there, I began shifting my attention off the myriad external cues and variables of riding my bike, onto awareness itself. Within my new-found space of awareness, I was able to feel my presence as well as the presence of the people, objects, and space surrounding me. It struck me that everyone else was sharing this awareness of each other, too. Though a sea of individuals, the Chengdu cyclists and I moved effortlessly as an integrated unit, as if with a collective mind.

Feeling energy moving inside me, integrating somatically and energetically into a group, and being aware of awareness itself made me hungry to cultivate more of that in my life, as well as to share it with patients. Of all the modalities I've studied, from acupuncture to meditation, I have found Asian movement therapy, specifically dao yin, which is a doorway to spontaneous qigong, most easily enables me to explore my body-mind connection, be aware of awareness, and experience myself integrated into the whole, whatever the whole may be. To help you experience this, I've selected practices that integrate our parts (the limbs) with the whole, and our internal and external worlds: Lizard Runs Across the Water and Frog Shimmy.

CHAPTER 10

Lizard Runs Across the Water

By improving the flexibility and strength of your spine, this exercise can yield a more upright posture. The more you relax and breathe in this resting position, the more your spine will release and lengthen, resting more clearly on the floor.

The movement circulates energy and blood to and from the torso and the four limbs.

If relaxation is your goal, focus your attention on the soles of your feet while doing the movement. If you want to feel more energized, focus on your palms. Since your body might "travel" along your resting surface as you do this exercise vigorously, it's best to do this practice on the floor instead of the bed.

1. Rest in a comfortable supine pose (Figures 1–3). Please do a body and breath scan.

2. With your legs extended on the floor, open them wider than shoulder-width.

3. Extend your arms overhead, letting them rest on the floor. They too should be wider than shoulder-width. Your arms can be relaxed, with the elbows slightly bent or straight, whichever you prefer. Your palms face the sky. Notice your body is in an X shape (Figure 14).

4. Breathe naturally throughout this exercise.

5. Reach your right arm along the floor without lifting it, as if someone is stretching you further into the X shape.

6. Next, extend your left leg along the floor as if someone is stretching you further into the X shape. Notice how you have now stretched your body along a diagonal—up to the right and down to the left.

7. Now, slide your right leg along the floor without lifting it, stretching you further into the X shape.

8. Finally, extend your left arm again. Notice yourself elongated into the four directions of the X shape.

9. Continue this X-shaped stretching sequence: right arm, left leg, right leg, left arm. Explore moving as quickly as you can.

10. As you go faster, you might notice your body sliding over the floor like a lizard running over the hot desert sand or running along the water's surface. Move as vigorously as is comfortable. Focus on stretching without lifting the limbs from the floor.

11. Continue for at least one minute.

12. Stop and rest in the X shape and finish with a full body and breath scan. What, if anything, do you notice? Does one leg or arm feel longer or heavier? Do you feel symmetrical or not? Do you feel energy circulating in your body? It may feel like a tingle, warmth, or vibration.

Figure 14

CHAPTER 11

Frog Shimmy

The posture in this exercise opens the shoulders and hips, which are referred to as the Four Gates or Four Corners. It helps energy flow from the arms and legs to the fingers and toes. The side-to-side movement resonates with Shao Yang and activates Tai Yang (see Chapter 37) through the spine, which mediates our interaction with the external world. This movement can shake and open things up when we feel withdrawn or unsure how to move forward, have difficulty interfacing with the world, or feel bogged down with phlegm.

1. Rest in a basic supine pose (Figures 1–3) and do a body and breath scan.

2. Roll onto your belly. Stack your hands, palms down under your head, and place your forehead on the back of your top hand (Figure 5).

3. Separate your legs wider than shoulder-width apart. Bend your knees as if to touch the soles of your feet together on the floor, creating a diamond shape with your legs (Figure 15). If this movement is too difficult, position yourself as best as you can without straining.

4. Inhale and slide your upper body to the right in a crescent shape. Your right elbow will be moving toward your right knee. Simultaneously, draw your right knee to your right elbow. (You might notice that your left leg has come out of

the bent-knee position.) Feel the lengthening of your entire left side and the shortening of your right side (Figure 16).

5. Exhale and make the same sliding movement to your left side, forming a crescent shape to your left side. Feel the lengthening of your right side and the shortening of your left side. You've just completed one cycle of the movement.

6. Repeat this movement for a total of three or nine times depending on your stamina, inhaling as you slide to one side, exhaling to the other.

7. Come to rest. Roll back onto your back (Figures 1–3) and do a body and breath scan, noticing any sensations in your spine, hips, and shoulders, or anywhere else that calls your attention.

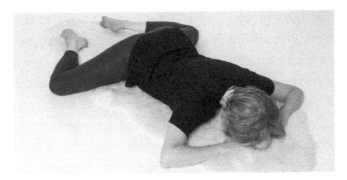

Figure 15

Figure 16

CHAPTER 12

Obstacle Illusion: The Yielding Quality of Water

Living by a river has given me ample opportunity to study water-falls. I go to the river when I seek solitude, when I need time to think through a problem, when I just want to listen to the music of the flow. Witnessing drop after drop separate from the whole, leap into the air for an instant, and then yield back to reunite with the source; the waterfall is a metaphor for life, death, and rebirth. Though we can look at the river as a symbol of transitoriness, it is also a symbol of permanence. The water never stops flowing, even when it reaches its lowest point—the ocean or an aquifer. The nature of that infinite flow is a comforting reminder that even though nothing stays the same, life, like the water, keeps on moving, ultimately returning to its source.

Early in 2020, I felt it was necessary to give more focused time and attention to writing this book. This led me to a vacation rental in Brevard, North Carolina, not too far from my home. The area is home to more than 250 waterfalls. Given the book's nature, my writing coach Sue suggested we get into the flow of the week by taking a walk to nearby Looking Glass Falls, an impressive 60-foot waterfall along the Davidson River.

After feeling the spray of the falls and smiling at the sight of exposed roots of shrubs dangling from the adjacent cliff face, we wandered further downstream. Eventually, we came to a mini waterfall. With dusk settling in, it wasn't easy to make out specific details of this water feature. What struck me was how the water glided, creating a velvety smooth, rounded contour, unlike the dramatic cascading waterfall upstream. As my eyes adjusted to the faint light, I noticed a large tree trunk had fallen across the entire breadth of the river, creating both dam and mini waterfall.

As I considered being like water, I thought about the "obstruction" the water encountered when the tree fell. If it were me, I might have felt inconvenienced by the imposition. It would have, after all, gotten in my way. Water has no such expectations. It simply encounters the trunk as part of the journey and moves on.

That's when an epiphany struck. Earlier in the month, I had experienced an unexpected and unfamiliar challenge while working on a project. A particular comment by a colleague triggered me. I felt disrespected, misunderstood, and undervalued. It took me by surprise; I was uncertain how to respond. Though I pointed out the falsity, I was unsatisfied without an apology. Clearly, we weren't seeing eye to eye.

Because I was in new territory, I consulted a trusted advisor. He recommended I let the perception be, as one might when encountering a snake along a wooded trail. He reminded me of Alan Watts' "The Story of the Chinese Farmer," counseling me to be like the farmer who stayed neutral—come fortune or disaster—no matter what other people's judgments were. He recommended I accept the circumstances as they were, let the judgments—mine and theirs— slip away, refocus, and continue accomplishing the program's objectives. He concluded by saying, "You never know what the ripple effect will be of any action; be neutral and see what happens next."

Given my hot-blooded conditioning, spiced with a sense of righteousness and indignation, not contending went against my grain. I wanted to pick that snake up and remove it from my path. Instead of reacting, however, I took my mentor's advice.

As I looked at the serene waterfall, I chuckled. There was no "me vs them" mentality between water and tree trunk, no insult or injury. The water didn't struggle to remove the trunk. Instead, the trunk became part of the flow, enhancing the terrain. I imagined it was responsible for giving rise to new micro-systems of flora and fauna. Clearly, everything here was in harmony. It dawned on me that if my mind were like water, I would have felt no need to contend with my colleague's perception. In fact, I wouldn't have perceived it as an obstacle in the first place. With that, I felt the weight of my struggle lift and tumble along with the water.

The lesson paid off. Because I yielded, my colleague and I were able to develop a camaraderie that allowed us to navigate the logistical challenges our program faced because of a global pandemic. Had I fomented conflict from our misunderstanding, we would not have been able to pivot, regroup, and co-create a rewarding path forward, one that allowed our program to continue to be of valued service to our community. As for their original perception of me and my hard feelings, our time working together washed those away and we developed a mutual respect for each other's skills and commitment. Upon reflection, this reminds me, even though it's soft and yielding, water's presence and persistence can wear away hard rock. As Rumi offered, when we move beyond our beliefs of right and wrong, good and bad, there's a neutral meeting ground.

It's eye-opening to experience an obstacle and notice our reaction to it. Even more enlightening is to see what happens when we don't contend with the opposition yet remain present to it. Here are two practices that give you the opportunity to do just that: Bamboo Twist and Free Me.

CHAPTER 13

Bamboo Twist

This is my go-to twist. Not only do I love how it makes me feel, it's also the one most requested by my students, especially those with back discomfort or hip and neck pain. This twist solidly rests in Shao Yang, helping us become more flexible, adaptable, and resilient. It addresses pelvic conditions related to the accumulation of fluid and blockages leading to uterine, ovarian, or prostate conditions, including cysts. It influences the eyes, benefiting our vision, literally and metaphorically, helping us to see things from different perspectives and expand our options.

1. Rest in a comfortable supine pose (Figures 1–3). Please begin with a body and breath scan.

2. Bend your hips and knees to stand the feet (Figure 3).

3. Cross your left leg over your right with your inner thighs touching. Notice the weight of the top left leg as it rests on your right.

4. Extend your arms in a T-formation at shoulder level, resting the backs of your hands on the floor.

5. Inhale and relax. This is your starting position for the next series of movements (Figure 17).

6. Exhale as you let your knees drop to the mat to the right (Figure 18). You may notice your head wants to turn to the

left. If so, go for it. Notice any sensations in your arms, ribs, waist, back, hips, and legs.

7. Inhale and push with your right leg to return to the starting position. If you turned your head to the left, allow it to return to the starting position as well.

8. Repeat two more times.

9. Now, inhale and hold the breath as you drop your knees and twist to the right. Stretch your fingers wide apart as they carry on resting on the floor.

10. When you get as far into the twist as you can go comfortably, exhale and allow your fingers and body to relax. You may notice your body moves more deeply into the twist.

11. Inhale, pushing with the right leg to return to the starting position. If you turned your head to the left, allow it to return to the starting position as well.

12. Repeat two more times.

13. For this last sequence, exhale the breath from your mouth with a whoosh sound and let your body flop into the twist. You may notice your head wants to turn to the left. If so, go for it.

14. Repeat two more times.

15. Return to supine position and do a body and breath scan. Notice if anything feels different. Does one side feel longer or heavier? Does one lung feel more expansive than the other or easier to breathe into?

16. Repeat the sequence on the other side with your right leg on top of your left.

17. Finish with a body and breath scan, noticing the length and

weight of your legs, any sensations in your ribs and lungs, or anything else.

Figure 17

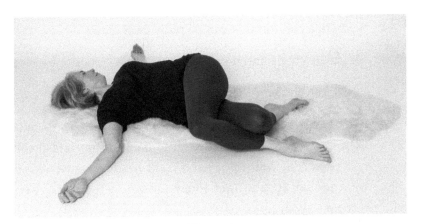

Figure 18

CHAPTER 14

Free Me

This exercise activates the Shao Yang and Tai Yang channels. Since this twist involves twisting with restrictions from being on your belly on the floor, it can yield a deeply expansive and grounding sensation.

1. Begin in a comfortable supine position (Figures 1–3).

2. Please do a body and breath scan.

3. Roll onto your belly into a comfortable prone pose (Figure 4).

4. Place your right hand, palm down, on the mat beneath your face. Turn your head to the right, placing your left cheek on the back of your right hand. Your head is positioned so you can look at your right elbow. Let your left arm carry on resting by your left side.

5. With your inner thighs and knees together, bend your knees and raise your feet together, with the shins perpendicular to the mat and the tops of your thighs resting on the mat. This is your starting position (Figure 19).

6. Inhale.

7. Exhale and drop the "bound" legs and ankles toward the left along an arc. As best you can, keep the ankles and legs together, as if bound, to prevent them from sliding back and

forth as you move. This can be a challenging movement. Move to the best of your ability, even if that ability is simply to imagine yourself doing the movement. Depending on how much you can move, your right thigh may come off the mat (Figure 20).

8. Inhale back to the starting position.

9. Repeat two more times.

10. Inhale and hold the breath. Notice where you feel added tension in the body as a result of holding the breath.

11. Now, drop the "bound" legs and ankles toward the left. When they get as far as they can, exhale and relax further into the twist. Notice if you feel any tension releasing and where that release happens.

12. Inhale back to the starting position.

13. Repeat two more times.

14. Inhale in the starting position.

15. Exhale and lift your head and right arm, keeping your left cheek on the back of your right hand, as you turn your head and eyes to look over your right shoulder. Drop your legs to the left as in the previous movement (Figure 21). If possible, coordinate the drop of your legs to the left with the lift and turning of your head and eyes to the right. Do your best, even if that means imagining yourself doing the movement. What are you like as you do this movement? Notice if any thoughts or emotions arise in response to the restrictions of the posture. If so, notice the type of thoughts—judging, critiquing, curious, for example—or emotions? Just notice and let them pass.

16. Inhale back to the starting position.

17. Repeat two more times.

18. Inhale in the starting position.

19. Exhale, and with a whoosh of the breath out of your mouth, lift and twist your upper body to the right and drop your legs to the left.

20. Inhale back to the starting position.

21. Repeat two more times.

22. Come to rest in a basic supine pose and do a body and breath scan, noticing the effects of the movement. When you feel complete, return to basic prone position.

23. Repeat the entire exercise to the other side.

Figure 19

Figure 20

Figure 21

CHAPTER 15

Equine-imity

My first mentor in mindful movement was a horse.

I was a fifth grader at a private Catholic school when I began riding as a form of therapy. My classmates' parents were white-collar professionals or successful entrepreneurs. My parents, on the other hand, had emigrated from Italy, and had thick accents and little formal education. Socio-economically, I didn't fit in. To add to my woes, my penchant for daydreaming often got me into trouble. I'd get called on and have no clue what the nun had been lecturing about. I still remember one assignment where I was supposed to write about Christopher Columbus. I made up most of what happened in his life based on my fantasies about his upbringing in a town near where my parents had grown up. Not only was I punished by the nuns for my flights of fancy, I was also teased by my classmates.

Recognizing I struggled in school and sensing my unhappiness, my mother, who knew I loved horses, gifted me with horseback riding lessons at a stable near the school. The best part of the week was tearing off my school uniform, pulling on my jeans and riding boots, and running as fast as I could to the stable.

At my first lesson, I was introduced to Black Horse, a tall horse with a sleek, black coat who emanated a gentle, seemingly wise nature. I was ready to jump on, but my riding instructor Becca, Black Horse's owner, had other plans for me. She showed me how to muck out his stall and groom him. Given Black Horse's mass, Becca gave me strict guidelines on how to move about the stall to avoid spooking him. Even though I was not one to focus well and follow directions, I somehow knew I had to heed her guidance to remain safe. While I had no idea why she felt it was important to teach me the different parts of a horse's body, I listened and learned. Then, I cleaned the tack. Having not ridden, I went home dragging my heels. As disappointed as I was, I didn't complain, because the entire time I was in his presence, I was moved by Black Horse's peace and, dare I say, kindness. I wanted to go back.

During the second lesson, I learned the parts of the bridle and saddle. I was instructed, again, to groom Black Horse. Heeding Becca's advice, I was mindful not to cross too closely behind him as I gently yet efficiently picked the mud from his hooves and brushed his luxuriously smooth hair. I noticed his dreamy aroma and breathed it in deeply, over and over. He smelled sweet, earthy, and slightly pungent. The warm, easy feeling I had in my belly when I was near him drew me to him even more. As eager as I was to ride, I was allowed no more than to muck out the stalls and go home.

When I arrived for my third lesson, I was excited to learn I would ride Black Horse. The fluttering feeling in my belly was a combination of fear and joyful anticipation. Becca instructed me on how to set the saddle and then wait for his out-breath before tightening the girth. After she demonstrated how to gently fit the bit into Black Horse's mouth, I put the bridle on him. Finally, after receiving careful instruction on how to mount him, I threw my leg over the saddle. I was up.

Being in that saddle gave me both a whole new perspective and a sense of accomplishment. My patience and focus had paid off. Best of all, I felt as if I had a new friend and was eager to get to know him better as we worked together.

As I adjusted my hands on the reins, Becca emphasized that a horse's mouth is sensitive. Black Horse would behave according to what he felt through the bit—where I wanted him to go, when I wanted him to accelerate, slow, and stop. She informed me that if I sent mixed messages or handled the reins carelessly, he'd be confused about what I was asking him to do. Becca let me know Black Horse was patient; other horses, if given mixed messages from the rider, might become annoyed and rebellious, even to the point of bucking. She also let me know I could sense his state of mind through his response via the reins.

Now, as I sat in the saddle, I realized there was so much to remember. In addition to how I communicated through the reins, I learned how my body language would also influence his actions. I admitted I felt a little insecure wondering how Black Horse would respond to me. Becca then explained the reason I spent the first two sessions mucking out the stall and grooming him. It was to build a trusting relationship that would allow him to "read" me. First and foremost, the feeling Black Horse had for me and I had for him would ultimately influence his behavior. She assured me he was relaxed in my presence and followed me with his attention, a sign I'd have a good ride.

During those first few walking laps around the outdoor ring, I became aware of how his body felt moving beneath me, the warmth, the rhythm, our collaboration, the new perspective. Black Horse sensed how I felt through the squeeze of my heels, the tension in my hands on the reins, my seat and thighs on his back and sides, the sound of my voice, and even my breathing. In my concern for Black Horse and wanting to connect with him, I was becoming more aware of what I was feeling in my body, more aware of thoughts in my mind and where I put my general attention. To be present for him, I had to be more aware of myself.

As my skills progressed, Becca invited me to leave the ring and explore more challenging terrain. Before allowing me to embark on my first trail ride through a thick wood, she explained that in addition to being aware of the messages Black Horse and I were sending each other through the reins and our movements, I needed to pay attention to the environment. For example, I needed to expand my attention to notice animals that might spook him, as well as fallen tree limbs and rocks that might make him stumble. My focus now encompassed my physical sensations and awareness of my thoughts, in addition to details like air temperature, the sounds of the babbling brook, rustling leaves, and light patterns. At the same time, I was aware of Black Horse's ease, tension, and breathing.

An awakening occurred when we first transitioned from the choppy bounce of a trot to the lilting rhythm of a canter. Going faster required even more trust in our connection and communication than before. I could feel Black Horse lift us up off the ground, airborne and weightless for a moment, and then set us lightly back down to earth, feeling our weight again. It was as if my senses were fully awakened. The sound and rhythm of his beating hooves, the warm and expansive feeling in my chest and belly, the tingle from the moving air brushing on my hands and face, the crisp aroma of autumn, the huff and puff of his breathing, and the vastness of the manganese-blue sky all came into crystal-clear focus simultaneously. The surface ripples of my worries and stresses from my day at school faded completely. As if by grace, my attention shifted from the numerous individual sensory details into an expansive sense. The line between me and Black Horse completely blurred. So perfect was our union, I felt as if I could have let go of the reins. It was like moments I've experienced at the ocean, in the early morning just before dawn, when the water is perfectly calm. Not only can I see through to the bottom, I can also see my reflection and the sky above. For an instant, I experience myself and everything around me simultaneously, as one.

Experiences of embodied presence, like the one I had cantering with Black Horse, help me connect to the essence of who I am. I've tended to want to hang on to those experiences and relive them, over and over, in an attempt to reconnect with myself. However, thinking the experience itself is my essence is like believing the moon is the source of its light.

Eventually, I left the nuns and my old school. I had to say goodbye to Black Horse. I stopped riding. Even though that experience was profound, somewhere along the way I completely pushed the memory and awakening aside. As I describe in these essays, I went searching for myself in a variety of ways throughout my adulthood. It's kind of humorous—all the complicated and expensive ways I went about trying to just meet and understand myself. All I ever had to do was to stop and pay attention in the moment.

Mindful movement continues to be an essential resource for me in cultivating my relationship with myself and others. One of the first things I do when attuning my attention to cultivate embodied presence is to check in with my senses and notice the details of life. This simple act is a primer for turning my attention to the light of my essence.

Here, I offer three dao yin exercises designed specifically to help you attune your sense of sight, sound, smell, taste, and touch to cultivate embodied, mindful presence in the moment: Head Roll and Release, Opening the Doorways to the Earth, and Opening the Windows of Heaven. Enjoy!

CHAPTER 16

Head Roll and Release

This movement is designed to release the neck and open up your sensory organs of the head and face (vision, hearing, smell, taste, touch). Because it can be quite intense, I recommend proceeding gently and mindfully, paying attention to any discomfort. If you experience dizziness, nausea, or headache, either do the movement more gently and slowly or please stop the physical movement and simply imagine yourself doing it.

This practice can release tension in your jaw, neck, shoulders, and low back. It can also benefit the trigeminal nerve and its sensory-motor relationship to the eyes, sinuses, teeth, and jaws. I recommend it to patients to address neuropathic pain.

1. Start with a body and breath scan in supine pose. Look at Figures 1–3 and select the one that feels most comfortable for you. If this changes during the exercise, feel free to explore one of the other options.

2. Place your left palm on your forehead.

3. Place your right hand behind your head, with the palm cradling the base of your skull.

4. Let your elbows release toward the mat, feeling the stretch across your chest and shoulders (Figure 22).

5. Inhale.

6. As you exhale, use your left hand to gently push your head to the right as if you had the intention of touching your right ear to your right shoulder. As your left shoulder blade moves in an arc along the floor and the elbow in the same arc parallel to the floor, you may notice a stretch along your left shoulder blade, side ribs, neck, and base of your skull (Figure 23). Please note: It's common to make the mistake of turning the head so the chin moves toward the right shoulder (Figure 24).

7. Inhale and pull your head back to center.

8. Repeat two more times, pushing and tilting your head to your right side on the exhalation and returning to center on the inhalation.

9. From center, exhale and push your head once again to the right.

10. Inhale, pulling your head back through center and continue in that same motion to pull your head to the left, in the same arc formation, moving your left ear toward your left shoulder (Figure 25). Remember to avoid turning the head so the chin moves toward the shoulder (Figure 26).

11. Continue rolling your head side to side, like a windshield wiper, exhaling through center to the right, inhaling through center to the left. Notice where your movement is easy and where it is limited. Do you notice any stiffness in your neck? If so, where? Do you hear any crackling sounds? Typically, they are indicative of something benign.

12. With your hands in the same position, inhale as you rest in the starting position.

13. Hold your breath as you rotate your head side to side in the same manner as you did in the previous movement (like a windshield wiper).

14. When you can't hold your breath any longer, exhale through your mouth with a whoosh as you push your head in the arc to the right.

15. Return to supine pose and do a body and breath scan. Feel the weight of your head. Notice if your head is leaning more to the left, or more to the right, or if you feel it is in a neutral space. Notice the effects of the movement, i.e. sensations in the head and neck.

16. Now, reverse the placement of your hands on the back of your head and forehead (right palm on forehead and left hand cradling the head).

17. Repeat steps 5–15, moving in the opposite direction.

18. When you've completed the movements, do another body and breath scan. Now that you've completed the movements on both sides, notice if one shoulder is heavier than the other. If so, is it on your dominant or non-dominant side? Since this exercise impacts your sensory organs, engage your eyes by slowly looking around the room. Note what colors, shapes, or textures you see. Tune in to your hearing, noticing any sounds, nearby and then beyond, identifying their volume, rhythm, tone.

Figure 22

Figure 23

Figure 24

Figure 25

Figure 26

CHAPTER 17

Opening the Doorways to the Earth

This movement opens up acupuncture points, channels, and physical regions we relate to grounding and our connection to the earth, namely the pelvis, groin, lower abdomen, back, and legs.

When we turn the toes in toward each other, we activate Yang Ming (see Chapter 37). Turning the toes away from each other resonates with Tai Yang. The back-and-forth twisting relates to Shao Yang and helps to open blood circulation in the pelvis, low back, and groin. Since it affects all three of the leg yang channel systems, this is a good practice for restoring balance in your musculoskeletal system. If you find your movement is restricted, either in one or both directions, there may be an energy block in the groin or a Yang Ming channel. Such a block can lead to menstrual, prostate, uterine, ovarian, urinary, or intestinal issues. This practice is also used to overcome addictions, as it can affect our attachment (Yang Ming) to vices. Additionally, working the legs in this way can help to resolve knee pain.

1. Rest in a comfortable supine position (Figures 1–3).

2. After completing a body and breath scan, please remove any support from behind the knees and place your legs wider than shoulder-width apart (Figure 27). This is your starting position.

3. As you inhale, rotate your legs and feet to drop your toes to the right (Figure 28).

4. Exhale and return to the starting position.

5. Repeat two more times.

6. As you inhale, turn both feet to the left.

7. Exhale back to the starting position.

8. Repeat two more times.

9. As you inhale, turn both feet to the right. Then, as you exhale, turn both feet to the left. Move as fast as you can, like a windshield wiper. Create a rhythm of breath and movement. Continue for about 30 seconds. If you get tired, please stop and rest.

10. Come to rest and observe whether one leg feels longer, looser, or heavier.

11. Inhale.

12. Exhale, keeping your knees straight, if possible. Turn your legs and feet so that your little toes fall toward the mat (Figure 29).

13. Inhale, keeping your knees straight, if possible. Turn your legs and feet so that your big toes fall toward the mat (Figure 30).

14. Continue in this manner, exhaling to turn your legs and feet out and inhaling to turn them in. Create a rhythm of breath and movement, moving as fast as you comfortably can for 30 seconds. If you get tired, please come to rest.

15. Once you've completed the movement, rest and observe any sensations in your feet, legs, hips, groin, and low back.

16. Gently and slowly turn your legs and feet in and out again, noticing if one direction feels more restricted than the other. If so, can you locate where the restriction is?

17. Rest and do another body and breath scan.

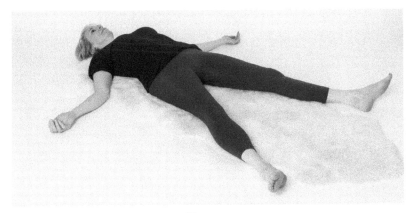

Figure 27

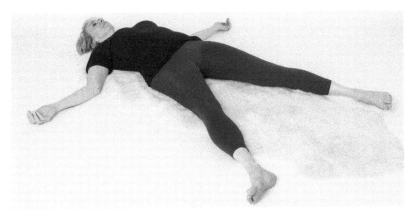

Figure 28

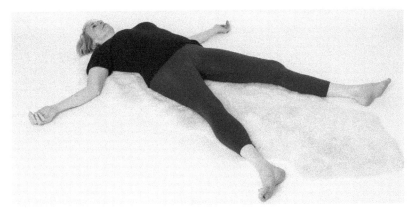

Figure 29

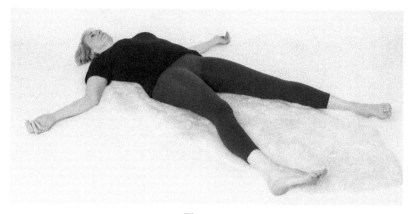

Figure 30

CHAPTER 18

Opening the Windows of Heaven

Windows of Heaven is a grouping of points located on the upper arm and chest, neck, and base of the skull. These points conduct energy to and from the torso and the head. Windows of Heaven points benefit the sensory organs, have a strong influence on our mental-emotional wellbeing, and are useful in the treatment of headache, dizziness, and neck pain.

Important: Please note that the Head Roll and Release is a prerequisite to this practice.

1. Rest in a comfortable supine position (Figures 1–3).

2. Please begin with a body and breath scan.

3. Place your palms facing toward your outer thighs with the thumbs pointing toward the ceiling and outer edges of your pinkies resting on the floor (Figure 31). This is your starting position.

4. Inhale.

5. Exhale and turn your hands to the right. Your right hand will be palm up while your left hand is palm down (Figure 32).

6. Inhale and move your hands back to the starting position.

7. Exhale and rotate your hands to the left. Your right palm is down while your left palm is up.

8. Inhale and return to the starting position.

9. Continue in this manner, flopping back and forth, and increasing your speed if this is comfortable. Breathe naturally as you move. If this creates discomfort, move at a pace that works for you.

10. Continue for about 15 seconds. Now, pause and rest in the starting position. Notice any sensations in your hands, arms, and neck.

11. Inhale, this time rotating both hands so the backs of your hands are on the mat and palms are up (Figure 33).

12. Exhale and rotate your palms down on the mat (Figure 34).

13. Continue in this manner, rotating your hands, palms up and then down, and increasing your speed if this is comfortable. Breathe naturally as you move. If this creates discomfort, move at a pace that works for you.

14. Continue for about 15 seconds. Now pause and rest in the starting position.

15. Please rest for a body and breath scan. Notice any sensations in your hands, arms, and neck. Does one side feel longer? If so, is that the dominant or the non-dominant side? Tune in to your sense of sight and hearing once again, naming the qualities of what you see and hear. Also, check in with your sense of smell and the taste in your mouth, noticing aromas or flavors.

Figure 31

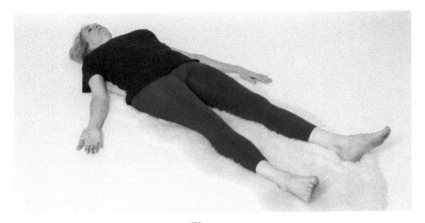

Figure 32

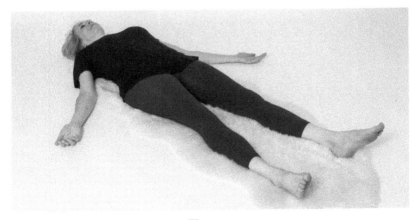

Figure 33

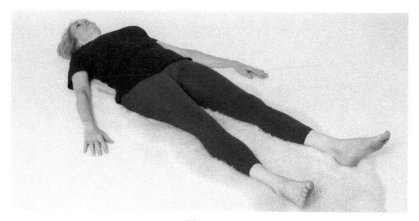

Figure 34

CHAPTER 19

The Purity of Water

Several times a week, I walk up a steep hill to visit a spring just up my country road. The cold, crystal-clear water flows from rock surrounded by verdant rhododendron and mosses. From the pristine spring, the water crosses underneath our road and makes its way across an old dumping ground where it then spills into the South Toe River about 100 feet below.

Watching the spring water emerge reminds me of how we initiate our life's path with purity and innocence. Just as this pure spring water can get murky or polluted as it moves through the terrain on its journey to the sea, our own waters get muddy as we move through our lives. Sometimes, we yearn to get back to that innocence. How do we redeem ourselves? According to Confucianism and Daoism, one way is by living ethically and according to our virtues.

I could be a poster child for muddying the water. For a few decades, my recurrent stumbling point was my irresistible attraction to romantic love. How I responded to that attraction was problematic because I was married, and my husband was not the sole object of my romantic desire. While I loved and cared for him, I fell deeply in love with an acupuncture college classmate. Over the years, other attractions followed, some more damaging than others.

Since my desire centered around love, it was easy to justify what I was feeling and doing. After all, to my mind, love was pure and always good. I didn't mean to hurt anyone; I was simply expressing love and tenderness in my own personal, spontaneous way. In reality, I was breaking my marriage vows and my husband's heart.

Not wanting to cause suffering to those dearest to me, or to myself, yet unable to stop myself from acting on my desires, I eventually sought the counsel of someone renowned for his steady presence and wisdom.

My dear friend and classmate Dave recommended his therapist. Over the years, I had heard many intriguing accounts of Dave's therapy sessions, which incorporated psychotherapy, hypnotherapy, yoga asana, philosophy, breathing exercises, and mindfulness meditation.

Dr. G. had been a WWII fighter pilot and prisoner of war who overcame paraplegia through yoga. Years of intense training and overwhelming adversity gave him the ability to be perfectly present. It was immediately clear that only honesty and sincerity were going to work in his presence.

We got down to business the moment he opened the door. In the midst of leading me through a series of movement and breathing exercises that required great focus, Dr. G. asked me what I had been seeking from my extramarital affairs. Because my conscious mind was occupied by the exercise, it didn't have the opportunity to censor what bubbled up from my subconscious.

The revelation was that I had been here before. Just as I had sought years before through my drug use, I yearned for something more—a connection to something greater than myself. Even though I knew from yoga, meditation, and Chinese medicine that the love I sought was with myself, I went looking for it in romantic relationships with others. In my attempt to find that love, I wound up destroying what I had.

Clear that I'd had an "aha" moment, Dr. G. moved his chair a little closer to me. Leaning in, but still at a comfortable distance, I could feel the magnitude of his powerful presence. With his soul-piercing eyes, he looked straight into mine and said with a soft, lilting voice as if he were talking to an innocent child, "You will never find fulfillment by obtaining the objects of your desires. It's not in the objects. You'll have to discover where true fulfillment lives and experience it for yourself."

The key to navigating my desires and being able to discover where fulfillment actually lives, according to Dr. G., was to focus on cultivating my virtues and mastering ethical living. Per his instructions, I began following the five abstinences (yamas—things not to do) and observances (niyamas—things to do) put forth in Patanjali's *Yoga Sutras* (see "Illustrations" at the end of the book). These are thought of as the Ten Commandments of yoga.

Honoring these commandments consistently brought up so much resistance. I had always been impetuous. Sometimes, I just wanted what I wanted when I wanted it. Putting the brakes on my desires felt too confining.

Eventually, I left Seattle, but I kept working with Dr. G. by phone. Occasionally, I flew to Seattle to see him in person. After a few years, I could tell he was starting to lose his patience with me because of my resistance to letting go of behaviors that kept getting me in trouble. To help keep me moving forward, he simplified my yama and niyama assignment to three practices.

The first was to focus on surrendering to a force greater than anything tangible—call it consciousness, or awareness, or God. He instructed me, when I was aware I was trying to control something or make a situation go my way, to reflect on what I was trying to get out of the situation. What was of importance to me? Peace? Safety? Love? Freedom? Connection? Once I recognized what I really yearned for, I would then say to myself, "Let go. Let God." It took some practice, but when I was able to do that, and mean it, I felt myself become unburdened.

Cultivating contentment in the present moment came next. For this, he recommended a daily gratitude practice. When I wanted to look at my relationship in a glass-half-empty way, I shifted my focus instead to one of the many beautiful attributes of our life together—our mutual sense of humor, our common values, our love of nature and family. Dr. G. asked me to act on my gratitude through gestures of loving-kindness. When doing this exercise, it dawned on me how self-centered I had actually been.

Finally, he sternly advocated getting to know myself better through vigilant self-reflection and self-inquiry. In other words, be ruthlessly truthful with myself, noting my thoughts and seeing my rationalizations for what they were.

Knowing I hated myself for my transgressions, Dr. G. added it was essential to forgive myself for my past actions. That hatred would hold me in a pattern, leading me to continue to repeat my mistakes. To forgive myself, he suggested I offer myself compassion. No one else, he emphasized, could do the work for me. He was also clear I'd never be satisfied while looking for love and connection outside of myself. Knowing he had offered the best guidance he could, he set me on my path, reminding me to invoke his presence and steel my resolve to follow the ethical living practices if I ever needed him.

One thing I've learned from my own experience and witnessing how others dance with virtues and vices, is how often we get pulled back into the very thing we want to change. The practices help me become more compassionate about that, not only to myself but toward others as well. Forgiveness, which once felt impossible to offer because I didn't feel worthy of it myself, is now much easier to give and receive.

Even after more than 20 years spent working on ethical living, which included divorce and remarrying, my desires still occasionally held dominion. In addition to working with Patanjali's ethical living practices, I started exploring a Confucian-based healing system, called Shan Ren Dao, translated as The Way of the Virtuous Person, which was developed in the late 1800s by Master Wang Fengyi. Wang Fengyi taught how to honestly look within, meet our inner, divine nature, and translate virtue into action. According to him, we are either guided by our virtues—namely benevolence, wisdom, propriety, integrity or faithfulness, and uprightness—or our vices. Reflecting on my experience, I liken my vices to the weeds in my garden, which rob nutrients and act as the roots of dis-ease and suffering. Thanks to Shan Ren Dao, I learned how to pull the weeds and nourish the roots and seeds of virtue.

For me, Shan Ren Dao has been both stabilizing and enlightening. I began practicing through weekly meetings with Diane, a certified lymphatic therapist, mentor of ruthless truthfulness and kindness, and friend. I started seeing Diane for help with some health issues, which, according to Chinese medicine, shared roots with my sexual and romantic history.

In addition to bodywork, she and I did weekly co-counseling with our own version of Shan Ren Dao for a couple of years. Our sessions began with identifying a vice we each wanted to explore. My top two were my tendency to blame other people for the things that didn't go right or go my way, and my tendency to get easily annoyed with family members. Next, we looked to the action we could take to find the virtues associated with those vices. For example, to counter blame, I acknowledged that everything in my life has a cause and an effect. When I found myself getting annoyed, I looked to myself, to the things I did that might annoy others, and to the mistakes I have made. Learning to recognize my own imperfections is a humbling antidote to both blame and annoyance. The cherry on top is being able to acknowledge the good in all things, including the messes.

The combination of Diane's manual lymphatic drainage work, which supported my body's detoxification process, and Shan Ren Dao felt like a purification. Over the course of several sessions, I cried what felt like an ocean of tears, helping me release years of pent-up sorrow, guilt, and regret.

Thanks to my work with Dr. G. and Diane, my penchant for desiring greener grass and stirring up pain and suffering for myself and others has fallen nearly completely away. I feel increasingly purified through the process of attending to my virtues and living ethically. Dr. G. was right. Fulfillment lies not in attaining objects of my desires but cultivating and living my virtues, resting in contentment, and loving myself as much as I love others.

Most of us have experienced how our choices and actions can get us into deep water—either mucky or clear. In Chinese medicine, our cognitive ability to weigh what's best for us and separate the pure from the impure relates to the small intestine. The small intestine, in turn, relates to our eyes and shoulder blades, which influence what we can put in our reach and manipulate; in other words, our choices and actions. Locust Looks East and West is an ideal exercise to affect the small intestine in its role of purification. Since our breathing process is also a way to detoxify, we'll explore Panning for Gold, which activates the diaphragm, and Welcome Breath to help open and expand the lungs.

CHAPTER 20

Locust Looks East and West

This stretch activates the Shao Yang and Tai Yang channel systems as well as the low back, hamstrings, and calf muscles. It can be excellent for paralysis or numbness in the lower body. Since Tai Yang can positively affect our immune response, this is a good practice for health during cold and flu season.

The cheek resting on the back of the hand stimulates the cheekbone. Our sensory orifices are ordered around the cheekbones. Moving the scapula also stimulates the sensory organs. This movement can address issues with any of the sensory organs, like jaw pain, oral herpes, runny nose, conjunctivitis, or ringing in the ears.

The Windows of Heaven points you worked in the previous essay are activated with this exercise. Inhaling while lifting the upper body also opens the lungs.

1. Begin in a comfortable supine position (Figures 1–3).

2. Please do a body and breath scan.

3. Roll onto your belly into a comfortable prone pose (Figure 4).

4. Place your right hand, palm down, on the mat beneath your face. Turn your head to the right, placing your left cheek on the back of your right hand. Your head is positioned so you can look at your right elbow. Let your left arm continue resting by your left side (Figure 35). This is your starting position.

5. Inhale and lift just the right elbow and forearm off the mat as far as is comfortable, leaving your palm on the floor. Your cheek continues resting on the back of the right hand.

6. Exhale and return your right elbow and forearm to the mat.

7. Repeat two more times, becoming aware of the muscles that help you make this movement.

8. Inhale and lift your upper body (head, chest, and right arm) off the mat as far as is comfortable. The left cheek continues resting on the back of your right hand as you raise up. Do your best to keep your right forearm parallel to the mat. Turn your eyes to the right as if to look at your left foot or tailbone area. You may not be able to see that far; just turn your eyes as far as you can. Allow your left arm to continue resting on the mat.

9. Exhale and gently lower your head, chest, and right arm to the mat.

10. Repeat two more times.

11. Place your left palm or the back of your left hand onto your left thigh, hip, or low back, whichever is most comfortable (Figure 36). If it's not comfortable, leave your left arm resting alongside your body on the mat.

12. Inhale and lift your upper body (head, chest, and right arm) off the mat as far as is comfortable, looking back as if to see your left foot (Figure 37). You may not be able to see that far; just turn your eyes as far as you can. Become aware of the muscles that help you make this movement. Notice if you feel any restrictions in the movement. If so, where? Low back? Shoulder?

13. Exhale and come to rest.

14. Repeat two more times. Notice if your left leg raises reflexively.

If so, let your left leg or both legs lift as you raise the head, chest, and right arm (Figure 38).

15. If, for some reason, you are feeling pain, find the range of movement that works for you, even if that means just imagining the movement.

16. When you have finished, roll onto your back in a comfortable supine pose (Figures 1–3) and rest. Repeat the body and breath scan, noting how your body is resting on the mat along with any differences you are feeling between your left and right side. Notice, too, the weight and length of your limbs as well as any sense of heaviness or expansion in your body. Does one lung feel different from the other? There is no right or wrong; it's just about noticing what you feel.

17. Return to a comfortable prone position (Figure 4).

18. Repeat the entire previous sequence with your left arm bent and right arm by your side.

19. Return to a comfortable supine position and end with a body and breath scan. Please pay particular attention to your low back, neck, and shoulder blades. What do you notice, if anything, as you tune into your senses now?

Figure 35

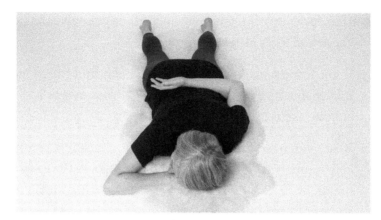

Figure 36

Figure 37

Figure 38

CHAPTER 21

Panning for Gold: Activating the Diaphragm

This movement is designed to activate your diaphragm, the dome-shaped abdominal muscle that separates the abdomen from the chest and affects our breathing. Because the movement can be quite intense, I recommend proceeding gently and mindfully, paying attention to any discomfort. If you experience dizziness, nausea, or headache, either do the movement more gently and slowly or please stop the physical movement and simply imagine yourself doing it.

Working the diaphragm can enhance the wellbeing of your liver, gallbladder, stomach, spleen, pancreas, heart, and lungs. It also has a strong effect on the vagus nerve, which can have a significant impact on how your body and mind respond to stress. This practice also relaxes the muscles next to the spine.

Some patients or students report that initially they can't direct their breath into their belly or chest. They can only feel the breath moving in one of those areas. If you find this to be true for you, no worries. Do your best to be curious and open to the possibility that, with practice, you'll have more connection and ability to breathe into these spaces.

1. Rest in supine pose. Look at Figures 1–3 and select the one that feels most comfortable for you. Please do a body and breath scan.

2. If you chose a supported supine position with knees resting on a bolster or knees bent with feet standing on the floor, check in and see if you could be comfortable extending the legs long, which is the preferred position for this exercise. If not, just rest in the position that is most comfortable. With repeated practice, you may eventually feel comfortable with your legs extended.

3. Take a deep breath into the lower abdomen, feeling the belly rise and expand on the inhalation (Figure 39).

4. Exhale. You may notice your belly deflating and moving toward the spine. Notice if you feel as if your spine elongates with the exhalation.

5. As you inhale, focus on allowing only the chest to expand. You can do this by stabilizing the belly and ribs (Figure 40).

6. Exhale and feel the chest deflate, dropping down toward the spine. Notice how the collarbones and shoulders move.

7. Inhale into your abdomen and hold your breath. This may feel as if you're holding a ball of air in your belly.

8. Hold the inhalation while collapsing the belly, pushing the ball of air into your chest. Notice how your chest rises as you roll that ball of air from belly to chest.

9. Exhale through your mouth with an "Ahhh" sound, allowing your chest to deflate.

10. Inhale into the abdomen again, forming that ball of air by holding your breath. Pump the ball into the chest, only this time do not exhale. Instead, continue holding the breath and push the ball of air back and forth between chest and belly.

11. As you hold the breath, continue pumping the ball of air from chest to belly and belly to chest. Pump as vigorously as

is comfortable. You may notice your head rocks in rhythm with your pumping.

12. When you can no longer hold the breath, return the ball to the chest, open the mouth, and exhale with an "Ahhh" sound, allowing your chest to deflate.

13. Rest and take a body and breath scan. Notice if a particular area—hips, chest, or head—feels heaviest. Where do you feel the breath most clearly now? What other physical sensations do you notice, if any?

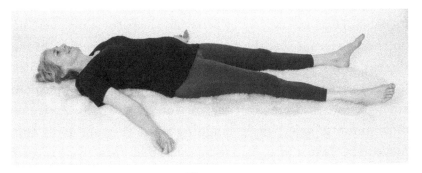

Figure 39

Figure 40

CHAPTER 22

Welcome Breath

As you practice Welcome Breath, I trust you'll come to understand its name. This exercise strengthens and clears the lungs. Resting on one side means that the ground restricts the movement of the ribs and lung on the floor-bound side. The other side compensates for the restricted air flow. The practice teaches us to breathe more efficiently when there is an obstruction or restriction. It is not uncommon to hear people coughing while they are doing this movement. Take it as a positive sign that they are activating their diaphragm and lungs when they cough.

I recommend this movement for patients who have respiratory tract infections or are otherwise having difficulty breathing. If you practice this while you are ill, exhale through the mouth. You can do the practice as described or you can simplify the movement, breathing in as you open the arm and chest into the twist, and then exhaling to return to the starting pose.

This movement affects the diaphragm, lungs, and Shao Yang.

1. Rest in side-lying pose on your right side (Figures 7–8). Extend both arms perpendicular to your chest with your right arm on the mat, palm up, and your left arm resting on top of it, palms touching (Figure 41). If it's not comfortable to rest your head on the ground, place a pillow under it for support. This is the starting position.

2. Inhale and lift your left arm until it's pointing straight up to

the ceiling, following the movement of your arm with your eyes and head (Figure 42).

3. Once there, exhale and continue opening your left arm, following the movement of the arm with your eyes and head (Figure 43). Go as far as is comfortable. Depending on your range of motion, you may find yourself contacting the mat with your left arm.

4. Inhale and return your left arm to that vertical position. Exhale as you slowly and gently return the left arm to the starting position. Once again, as you make the movements, let your head and eyes follow the movement of your arm.

5. Repeat two more times.

6. Back in the starting position, inhale and hold your breath. Lift your left arm and open it to the left, as far as you comfortably can. Follow the arm movement with your head and eyes.

7. When you reach your maximum twist to the left, exhale and relax in the twist. Notice if that release allows you to move more deeply into the pose. Whether you find your left arm is able to make contact with the mat isn't important; the point is simply to notice what you feel as you move.

8. Inhale and slowly return your left arm and palm on top of your right, following the arm movement with your head and eyes.

9. Repeat two more times, returning to the starting position. Exhale and rest.

10. From the starting position, inhale and hold your breath. Lift your left arm and open it to the left, as far as you comfortably can. This time, let your head remain still, *without* following the motion with your head and eyes (Figure 44). When you

reach your maximum stretch, exhale and allow your head and eyes to follow the twist to the left. Relax in the twist. Notice if this allows you to move more deeply into the pose.

11. Inhale and slowly return your left arm and palm on top of your right, following the arm movement with your head and eyes.

12. Repeat two more times. Exhale and rest.

13. Inhale in starting position. Exhale, flopping into the twist with your arm, head, and eyes, letting the breath rush out of the mouth with a whoosh. Move in a way that is easy and relaxed.

14. Repeat two more times.

15. Return to supine pose, and do a body and breath scan.

16. Does one lung feel more open? Does one side of your body feel longer, wider, heavier? Are you aware of any thoughts or emotions? Notice the weight of your head, shoulder, and hip, and the length of your arms.

17. Repeat the entire sequence on the other side.

Figure 41

Figure 42

Figure 43

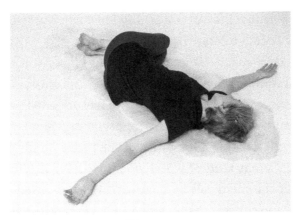

Figure 44

CHAPTER 23

Roll on River

What does it mean to be ageless, to be in harmony with the flow of time and the change of seasons? I started exploring this question when I was in my late 30s. Looking in the mirror, I could see time and life experience were shifting my youthful countenance. My hair had started turning grey, something I noticed shortly after my father's death a few months before.

The loss of my dad made me want to reconnect with my heritage. I was especially interested in regaining command of the language he and my mom spoke at home, the language I didn't want to speak as a young adult. With little effort, I was able to find an intensive language program at the University for Foreigners in Perugia. One day, while I was on break from classes, a staff person approached me. He asked if he could buy me an espresso. As we sipped, he inquired about my personal life. After learning I had a five-year-old son, he asked how I could tolerate having grey hair.

I was taken aback. "Do you want your young son to look up at you and wonder why his beautiful mother is old-looking?" this stranger asked. I didn't know whether to feel offended by his sexist rebuke or supported by this frank counsel. I told him I didn't want to put chemicals on my body. To this, he threw up his hands and exclaimed, "What kind of world would we have if Michelangelo cared about the chemicals in his paint?" He then asked me to join him at a piano concert that evening to listen to Mendelssohn's "A Midsummer Night's Dream." The intense beauty of the performance moved me into my own reflection. What's wrong with enhancing beauty? The next day I made an appointment to have my hair colored.

I continued coloring my hair for several years. In my mind, I equated looking old with being less relevant and less valued.

The more I thought about it, the more I realized how many remarkable grey-haired people caught my eye and sparked my intrigue because of their dynamism, flexibility, honesty, and strength. It dawned on me that it wasn't the wrinkles and grey hair that were the problem. That's just the narrative, I told myself. It was the underlying self-doubt and insecurity about my own value that was at issue.

I've often wondered—what effect do the thoughts of wanting to change myself because of a sense of insecurity, inadequacy, or irrelevance have on my body and quality of life?

In pondering this, I studied the research of Dr. Masaru Emoto, a Japanese doctor of alternative medicine. His passion was studying the effect of thoughts or environmental factors on the crystalline formation of water. As part of his research, he exposed containers of water to a word or thought and then studied the effect the word or thought had on the structure of the water crystals. When he offered water a positive word or phrase, like "happiness," "you are beautiful," "I love you," or "thank you," the water formed beautiful, ordered, intricate crystals when frozen. When exposed to words like "fool," "I hate you," or "it's no good," the water crystals were jumbled, hollow-looking, asymmetrical, or only partially formed.

I'm especially interested in his work because we humans are comprised of approximately 70 percent water. Might our thoughts about ourselves have an effect on that water? I feel certain the answer is yes. This is why mindfulness of thoughts and emotions feels so important to me.

How do I love and accept myself as I am? I've discovered I'm best able to do this when I let go of the narrative that my mind goblin spins—the one that says I haven't accomplished enough, I'm not successful enough, I'm not attractive enough. Instead, I turn my attention toward the things I appreciate about myself, like my kindness and compassion. In focusing on my positive attributes, I gain a firmer sense of my life's value and meaning.

In this phase of my life, I am more inspired and eager to continue learning about myself and my medicine, and to use what I learn to help others.

When I was younger, I had great adventures such as walking on lava tubes at midnight, a risk I would not take now because my life is not just about me, it's also about my family and community.

Now, my adventuring is focused inward. I can say, without a doubt, getting to know myself has been the greatest adventure yet. When I tune in, I recognize that my maturity and wisdom make me more effective, more focused on others and our common good, more confident, and more of a team player. I have a sense of peace and acceptance that had previously been absent. The more I connect with my strengths, the less I care about how others perceive me.

Thanks to this life's path, I understand my mission and I am actively making it unfold. I'm learning to use my time and energy wisely.

How I look now is a direct reflection of the path I've been walking. If you told me now to dye my hair, I'd have a moment of insecurity before brushing it off with a knowing smile.

To help us move into our future gracefully, I've chosen two practices. The first invites us to learn more about ourselves as we look to the future, Locust Looks Ahead. The second practice, Returning to the Core, focuses our attention on our center to build our core strength.

CHAPTER 24

Locust Looks Ahead

This prone posture moves into a backward bending pose, resonating with Tai Yang, strengthening the back. Stimulating the spine and vision, this pose helps us see the possibilities in front of us and engage with them. This practice is said to also benefit the teeth.

Locust Looks Ahead can be a challenging posture and movement. Take care to work within your comfort zone. If it proves too difficult, you can do it standing up by resting your chest and belly against a wall. For some, positioning the hands at the back of the head is not possible. Do your best within your comfort zone. If even that is too much, simply imagine yourself doing it.

1. Please rest in a supine pose (Figures 1–3). Please do a body and breath scan.

2. Roll onto your belly, resting face down in a prone position (Figure 4). If possible, place your arms behind you, resting your palms in the hollow of your low back (Figure 45). If that is not possible, remain in a comfortable prone pose (Figure 4, 5, or 6).

3. Inhale and slowly raise both legs completely off the mat, if possible, pointing the toes away from your head (Figure 46). If lifting both legs at the same time causes pain, or is not possible, feel free to do this movement one leg at a time, alternating sides. You may notice the leg that is not being

raised is pressing involuntarily into the mat. Notice what muscles are being engaged in order for you to lift your leg(s).

4. Exhale and return your leg(s) to the mat.

5. Repeat two more times. Notice, as you breathe in and lift—is one hip easier to lift? Rest, and notice if one leg feels longer than the other. If so, is it on the side of your dominant hand or non-dominant hand?

6. Place one hand over the other, palms down, on the floor under your head and rest your chin on the back of your top hand.

7. Inhale and lift just the upper body—chest, head, and elbows and arms—off the ground (Figure 47). If this is too difficult, just imagine yourself doing this movement. Again, notice what muscles are being engaged in order for you to lift your upper body.

8. Exhale and return to the ground.

9. Repeat two more times.

10. Rest your arms alongside your body. Place your head in whatever position feels right to you, with either your forehead or chin resting on the ground.

11. Interlace your fingers and place your hands on the back of your head, with your palms at the base of your skull. Make sure your thumbs are touching the sides of your index fingers and not tucked into your palms (Figure 48).

12. Feel the weight of your hands resting on your head without pressing down.

13. Inhale and lift your head to press into your clasped hands. If this is not comfortable, please remember to modify the pose or come to a comfortable resting position and simply

imagine yourself doing the movement. If you are comfortable, lift only your head, leaving your elbows and upper body on the ground (Figure 49). As you lift your head, you may notice the resistance from your arms. You may get the sense that your legs want to raise off the mat. Just notice this and allow them to remain on the floor.

14. Exhale and return your forehead or chin to the ground.

15. Repeat two more times.

16. Inhale. Keeping your palms on the back of your head, lift your head, elbows, arms, and chest off the ground as best you can (Figure 50). Notice what muscles you need to use to make that happen. Shoulders? Upper back? Neck? Lower back? Buttocks? Legs?

17. Exhale and return to rest.

18. Repeat two more times.

19. Inhale, and lift your head, elbows, chest, and also your legs off the ground (Figure 51). Your legs should be no wider than shoulder-width apart. Point your toes. Roll your eyes to look upward. Squeeze the buttock muscles.

20. Exhale and release down to the mat.

21. Repeat two more times.

22. Roll onto your back, resting in a comfortable supine pose (Figures 1–3). Please do a body scan. Reflect on how you positioned your head. Did you place your forehead on the backs of your hands (relating to more internal focus) or did you turn your head to one side (dominant or non-dominant)? Did you place your chin on the ground, as if to see the world ahead of you? Check in with your vision, as you slowly move your eyes, noticing the colors, shapes, and textures you see.

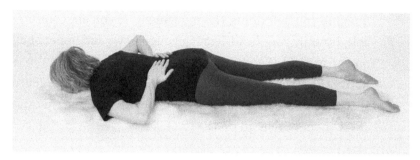

Figure 45

Figure 46

Figure 47

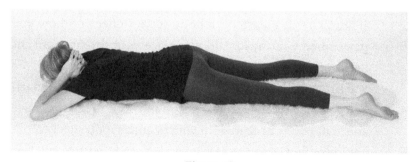

Figure 48

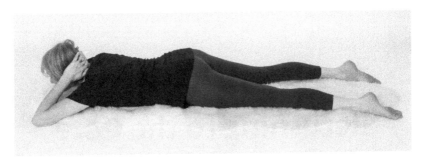

Figure 49

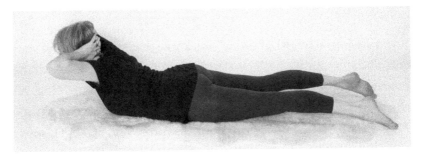

Figure 50

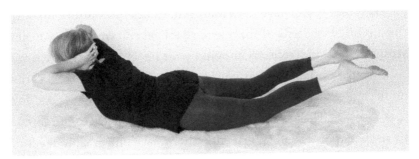

Figure 51

CHAPTER 25

Returning to the Core

If you are into strength training, you know that strengthening your core abdominal muscles is essential for a healthy back. Practicing movements that strengthen the abdomen belong to Yang Ming, yet the benefits transfer to Tai Yang. Metaphorically speaking, Yang Ming calls us inward to gather our resources and strength so we can extend outward.

This may be the most challenging exercise in this body of dao yin exercises. If you have neck and/or low back discomfort, do only the modified versions of this exercise for several weeks. As you get stronger with practice, try moving your heels further away from your buttocks. The further your heels are from the buttocks, the more challenging the practice will be. If you have neck issues, you may discover, with practice, you no longer need to use your hands to support your head. Work with the most comfortable level of modification for your neck and back, allowing the practice to evolve as you get stronger. If the practice proves too difficult at first, simply imagine yourself doing it.

When you wish to activate Yang Ming, choose either this practice or the Agony and Surrender in Chapter 31.

PART 1

1. Rest in basic supine position (Figures 1–3). If you are comfortable with your legs long, this is the preferred starting position.

2. Inhale and, with your shoulders resting on the floor, lift your head as if to look at your toes (Figure 52). If this bothers your neck, interlace your fingers and place your hands behind your head to support you as you gently raise your head (Figure 53).

3. Notice if your abdominal muscles are engaged as you raise your head.

4. Exhale and return your head to the mat.

5. Repeat three times.

6. Rest and notice where you feel your breath most clearly (belly, ribs, chest, head).

7. Rest with your head and shoulders on the mat.

8. As you inhale, engage your abdominal muscles to help you lift your legs a few inches off the ground. Try holding your legs as straight as possible with the intention of keeping your low back in touch with the floor. The goal is not to lift the legs as high as you can, just to lift them off the ground. If this is not possible or causes pain, do this exercise with your hips and knees folded to stand your feet. From this position, inhale, engage your abdominals, again with the intention of keeping your low back in touch with the floor, and lift your feet a few inches.

9. Exhale and return your feet/legs to the mat.

10. Repeat several times.

11. Rest in basic supine position and notice any changes in how

your body contacts the ground, as well as any other sensations. Do a breath scan, noticing where you feel the breath most clearly.

12. Inhale and lift your legs from the floor as you simultaneously tuck your chin into your chest and gently raise your head (Figure 54). If this bothers your neck, interlace your fingers and place your hands behind your head to support you as you gently raise your head. If this is not possible or causes pain, do this exercise with your hips and knees folded to stand your feet. With the intention of keeping your low back in touch with the floor, tuck your chin, and raise your chest and head as you simultaneously lift your feet a few inches.

13. Exhale and return your head and feet to the floor, slowly and with control, engaging your abdominal muscles.

14. Repeat three times, moving slowly and carefully.

15. Rest in supine position and notice any changes in how your body contacts the ground, as well as any other sensations. Since this exercise relates to the digestive system, tune in to your sense of smell and taste.

Figure 52

Figure 53

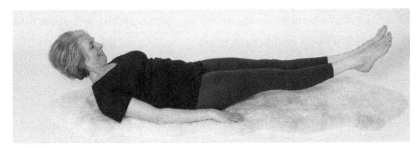

Figure 54

PART 2

1. Rest in basic side-lying position (Figures 7–8), on your right side.

2. As you inhale, straighten your lower legs so your entire legs are perpendicular to your torso (Figure 55).

3. As you exhale, bring your lower legs back into the basic side-lying position, as if you are trying to touch your buttocks with your heels.

4. Repeat three times.

5. Rest and notice what you feel.

6. This time, exhale as you stretch your legs to that perpendicular position in front of you while you simultaneously tuck your chin into your chest (Figure 56).

7. Inhale and bend your knees to return your heels toward your buttocks. At the same time, return your head to a neutral position.

8. Repeat three times.

9. Rest and relax in a supine position. Please do a body scan, noting changes, such as whether one side feels longer or heavier. Where do you feel the breath most clearly now?

10. Repeat the entire side-lying sequence on the left side. End with a body and breath scan.

Figure 55

Figure 56

CHAPTER 26

Unfolding

What is the point of life? I've asked myself this on days when I was filled with wonder and on those when I was filled with despair. I appreciate the Daoist concept that life is an unfolding of our divine purpose, our mission. That's easier said than done, though, when you aren't sure what your mission is and you don't know how to uncover it.

My mom's death gave me pause to consider the purpose and meaning of my life. Before we knew she had cancer, I had planned to go to medical school. The summer before my senior year, to prepare myself, I worked on a research project with my former pediatrician at a local hospital.

As much as I relished the science of medicine, I didn't appreciate that conducting medical research and doing rounds required viewing our newborn patients as subjects, reducing their experience and disease into an impersonal diagnosis, separate from their life beyond the hospital. In my heart, I knew I wanted a more holistic approach.

After weighing my options for completing my major requirements, I decided to shift focus from medicine to ecology. What drew me to ecology was how it investigates relationships within and between systems, reminding us how everything is connected to and influences everything else. I appreciated what naturalist John Muir (1911) had said: "When we try to pick out anything by itself, we find it hitched to everything else in the Universe." This philosophy resonated with me.

After graduation, I found work doing ecological research from Alaska to Antarctica for a couple of years before going on to graduate school. I was in my first semester at Rutgers University when Mom died.

Her death rekindled my interest in medicine. Just as I had experienced in the hospital with my internship, I witnessed her humanity being reduced to little more than a diagnosis and a treatment plan. I believed there must be some form of medicine that used an ecologically inspired framework and principles to restore and maintain health. I wanted to find that.

My dear friend Brenda Harvey, to whom this book is dedicated, showed me the way. Brenda worked at our local health center with a nurse practitioner who was fired up about Chinese medicine. With a twinkle in her eye and a broad smile, Brenda said she had a book for me to read: *The Web That Has No Weaver* by Ted Kaptchuk, which is about Chinese medicine. I was initially skeptical. What little I knew seemed more magical than medicinal.

Thankfully, Brenda had a special way of getting folks to reconsider their perceptions and positions. She reminded me I had used Chinese herbs in the past. Several years earlier, a clerk at a health food store recommended a Chinese herbal formula for help with a hormonal imbalance that hadn't resolved with traditional Western pharmaceuticals. I took the herbal formula out of sheer desperation. It worked so well, even my doctor wanted to know what I had taken.

I agreed to read the book. By the end of the introduction, I was hooked. There, before my eyes, was the ecological sensibility that seemed to be missing for me in Western medicine. Certain I had found the practice of medicine I had been looking for, I began researching Chinese medicine training programs. A few months later, I was studying at the Northwest Institute of Acupuncture and Oriental Medicine in Seattle.

No one could have been more surprised than I at finding a practice and philosophy that spoke to me on both an intellectual and spiritual level. Tapping into something that suited me so perfectly felt like grace. Even now, almost 30 years later, that feeling continues. This medicine has been my greatest teacher and, in that, a potent medicine itself.

I see my path, my mission, and myself unfolding more effortlessly and clearly. Incorporating mindful movement into my personal and professional practices has not only helped me come to know myself, it's also allowed me to help my patients come to a better understanding of themselves. Up until recently, it seemed practicing Chinese medicine was my mission. What I now understand is that awareness itself and an understanding of myself is actually what my life is about. The medicine is a vehicle for me to fulfill that mission and help others fulfill theirs.

Here we explore a movement that benefits the heart and kidneys, two organs central to understanding who we truly are. The heart is thought to be the residence of the spirit. By relaxing and expanding the chest to invite more breath, oxygen, and circulation, we can breathe possibility into our lives. The kidneys govern our courage and will to face who we are, with all our challenges, and work with the heart to help our mission unfold. It's thought the kidneys govern the realm of the subconscious. From their mysterious depth, concerns and fears bubble up for our review. From above, the light of the heart shines down into the mysterious realm of the kidneys, offering assurance, helping us to see our resources and strengths.

These two practices, Stretch the Bow and Fire and Water, help the heart and kidneys synch up and have a conversation. The first opens the heart and strengthens the back, which in Chinese medicine is considered the realm of the kidneys. The second puts the squeeze on the heart and kidney channels. When we relax, we'll see the effects these practices have on the chest and low back.

CHAPTER 27

Stretch the Bow

Stretch the Bow activates Tai Yang, our ability to look ahead, and our desires to interact. As it strengthens the back and promotes flexibility of the spine, it also stretches the front body, the terrain of Yang Ming.

Our transition from winter to spring is one of moving from hibernation and rest into action and growth. This position helps our energy move from spring's emergence into summer's blossoming. Please practice Stretch the Bow during the spring and summer months only.

1. Rest in a comfortable prone position (Figures 4–6).

2. Bend your knees to place your feet in the air. Your shins are perpendicular to the mat. This is your starting position (Figure 57).

3. Inhale.

4. Exhale and move your heels toward your buttocks (Figure 58).

5. Inhale and return your legs to the starting position.

6. Repeat two more times.

7. Exhale and move your heels toward your buttocks as you raise your head and chest and look up (Figure 59). If this creates

discomfort, move as much as you can comfortably, even if this means doing the movement in your imagination.

8. Inhale and relax to the starting position.

9. Repeat two more times.

10. This time, as you exhale and draw your heels toward your buttocks, lift both your head and chest, look up, and reach back and grab your ankles, if you can, and draw them toward your buttocks. Depending on your arm length, your elbows might be straight or bent (Figure 60). If this creates discomfort, move only as you comfortably can, even if this means just reaching your arms alongside your body, palms facing each other, as you draw the heels in. If this is too challenging for now, do the movement in your imagination.

11. Inhale and rest in the starting position.

12. Repeat two more times.

13. Come to rest on your back in a comfortable supine pose and do a body and breath scan.

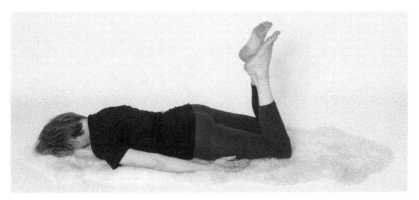

Figure 57

Figure 58

Figure 59

Figure 60

CHAPTER 28

Fire and Water

In Chinese medicine, every organ has a corresponding natural element. The heart resonates with fire, while the kidneys resonate with water. Squeezing and then releasing the arms in this exercise benefits the heart by relaxing the chest and allowing the chest cavity to expand, improving breathing capacity and blood flow. The heart is thought to be the residence of the spirit or mind. Squeezing and then releasing the legs benefits our kidneys, which are thought to be the foundation of our health. The combination of squeezing and releasing the arms and legs promotes communication between the heart and kidneys, which is essential for our cardiovascular health and is believed to be essential for our mental and spiritual health.

1. Rest in basic supine position with your knees bent and feet standing on the floor (Figure 3) and do a body scan.

2. Place your right hand on your left shoulder and your left hand on your right shoulder, with your left arm over your right (Figure 61).

3. With the back of your head resting on the ground, inhale and tuck your chin toward your chest, ultimately lifting your head off the ground. Go only as far as is comfortable.

4. Exhale and gently release your head back down to rest on the ground.

5. Inhale, tuck your chin, and lift your head to your chest. At the same time, tighten the muscles of your arms and press your hands to give your shoulders a gentle squeeze.

6. Exhale and release the squeeze and return your head to rest on the floor.

7. Repeat two more times.

8. Cross your right leg over your left leg, with your thighs touching.

9. Inhale and tuck your chin, lifting your head to your chest as you squeeze your arms. At the same time, lift your knees to your chest, squeezing your legs together (Figure 62).

10. Exhale and release your head and left foot back to the ground. Relax your arm and leg muscles.

11. Repeat two more times.

12. When you've finished, rest in supine pose with your legs extended and resting on the ground.

13. Breathe into and out of your chest, keeping your belly as still as possible.

14. Repeat two more times.

15. Breath into and out of your belly, keeping your chest as still as possible.

16. Repeat two more times.

17. Come to rest in a supine position and do a body scan.

18. Repeat the entire sequence with your right arm on top of the left arm and your left leg on top of your right leg.

19. When you come to the final rest, notice if you feel any sensations in your chest. If so, what are they like?

Figure 61

Figure 62

CHAPTER 29

The Water Cycle

Water's superpower is its ability to transition from solid to liquid to gas, and back again. It takes many forms, from the hardened ice I skated on as a kid, to the rushing milk-colored meltwater from the glaciers I crossed in Antarctica, to the dissipating clouds hugging the mountains of Hawaii's Kilauea Valley as I watched from the beach.

People don't transition as easily as water. We cling to our attachments of either what was, what is, or what we wish for in the future. Grappling with my attachments has been most acute when the transition is the death of a loved one.

For me, losing a family member or dear friend has come with intractable grief. I miss their physical presence. I also feel the loss of simple things like being able to pop in for a chat, ask for recipe details, share the bounty of each other's garden, cry on each other's shoulder, and laugh heartily over a glass of wine. When my parents died, I was bereft for decades. Part of my grief was regret for taking their generosity and ever-present support for granted. I felt bad for not having honored and thanked them enough for their love. I hadn't cherished them while they were alive. I suffered, knowing I would never get that time or opportunity back.

These decades of mindfulness study and practice have helped me mature and allowed me to understand the First Law of Thermodynamics, which states that energy may change form but is never destroyed. It is simply transformed and lives on.

The acute grief and regret finally let go once I recognized that my parents were always with me in spirit. It warms my heart to see my kids have some of their gestures and expressions. Because of this, loss feels like an opportunity to reconnect with myself and what's essential. This became clear when our dear cat Frisky died.

Frisky was no ordinary pet. Seemingly self-aware, calm, and unflappable, he was like a mirror for me when I was freaking out about little things. I could look at his serene countenance and realize I could drop the drama of whatever I was mentally and emotionally embroiled in and laugh at myself.

I think he liked being around me best when I was meditating. Frisky joined me each morning for my daily practice of movement, chanting, and meditation. He'd appear about 20 minutes after I started, around the time my thoughts stopped being so distracting and I could focus more clearly on the present. It felt like I was practicing with a dear friend who had more advanced skills than I.

Sometimes, he just sat nearby, looking relaxed and satisfied, with his eyes half closed, purring softly. If I was sitting on the floor poised in a mudra, meditating, I eventually noticed Frisky's gentle but rough tongue tenderly stroking the tips of my fingers. Next came the pressure of one paw, and then another, as he gingerly stepped into my lap and curled up into a purring ball. If I was doing a standing qigong practice outside, he sat next to my left foot when I was standing with my feet as wide as my shoulders. No matter what I was doing, he seemed to know the appropriate place to position himself and become part of my practice (or was I becoming a part of his?).

A colleague said it best—Frisky was a Zen master in cat's pajamas, always positive, quietly determined, compassionate, present, playful, kind, calm, and oh so sweet.

On his 14th circle around the sun, he began losing weight. He remained cheerful, tolerant, and loving. After several months, Frisky's weight loss was accompanied by wobbly walking. He'd disappear for long periods, somewhere in the woods, leading my children to say he was on his spirit journey, getting ready to leave this earthly realm. The vet recommended we make him as comfortable as possible or consider euthanasia. None of us wanted to put him down. Instead, we wanted to give him the opportunity to die in his own time and in his own way. For our part, we planned to be present for him with all our love and as much attention as he would allow us to give.

As the days went on, longer than any of us expected, he became as light as a feather, more bony, and less balanced. He eventually stopped sitting in front of the pantry where the cat treats were and stopped eating altogether. It was clear he wouldn't be with us much longer.

Knowing we would be present for his death in our home, I found myself looking back to childhood memories of how my mom modeled coping with death. When we were children, she took my brother and me to Italy once a year to visit family. If someone in our family was dying, my mother dressed us up and took us to their house.

The scene was always somber. There they'd be, dressed in black, propped with pillows on their bed, a far-off look in their eyes that made me think they were not solidly in our world anymore. Although broth or water mixed with wine was offered, they were most often rejected. We sat in relative silence or amidst hushed conversation for what felt like hours as family members came and went. We were simply there, all together, to honor, witness, reflect, and support.

That tradition of bearing witness to one's transition had firmly taken root and it resurfaced when my mom was dying. Although I was far away, and in the midst of my research obligations, I rushed through them and got home to be with her. Once at the hospital, I spent her remaining hours holding her hand and singing to her.

Here, sitting with her, being right in the moment, breath by breath, I felt such a sweetness between us. That had not been our usual way of relating. My mom was like a general. She wasn't overtly affectionate. Tender moments were few and far between. In that moment, however, her intense love was palpable.

The moment before she died, her face was illuminated as if by a soft light. She looked upward and smiled a serene, fulfilled smile. I can't quite explain what I witnessed next. It was as if her energy left her body through her head and rose up to heaven. In that moment, she looked peaceful and beautiful. It was a gift to see such radiance after watching how the cancer treatments ravaged her. I felt privileged to witness her transition. It helped me feel less afraid, more accepting, and even curious about my own ultimate transition.

As for Frisky, on what we imagined to be his final day, we surrounded him with healing stones and flowers from the meadow. We played sacred chants. I prayed over him for peace, freedom, and ease, trusting he had learned all he needed in this lifetime. We thanked him for his genuine presence, the love he gave, and the life lessons he taught us. Even as I felt great sorrow, knowing I'd miss my dear friend and mentor, I wanted him to be free.

Though still breathing, albeit shallowly, his consciousness was no longer in his body. On his last night, just before we all went to bed, we checked on him. He was completely still. We could neither detect his breath nor feel his pulse. We watched him for several minutes and concluded he was dead.

As we said goodbye, my daughter Gina and I stroked him the way he liked most and thanked him again for his blessings. It took us by surprise, and actually freaked out Gina, when he heaved a big breath, several in a row in fact, and began quiet, regular breathing. I realized we'd have to leave him alone or else he'd come back to us.

Though he's physically not here, Frisky continues to influence us through tender memories and a palpable sense of his presence. The simultaneous absence yet undeniable presence reminds me of a line I once read: "Can walking through a cloud not drench you as if you had plunged yourself into the ocean?"

A few days after Frisky's transition, my family wanted to get kittens. I was mourning and didn't think I was ready to make that step. In the past, my sorrow would have gripped me to such a degree that I wouldn't have been able to open up to the possibility of loving someone or something as much as the one I had just let go. But this time, something was different. I felt complete thanks to the process of letting Frisky go.

I'm in love with our kitties—their playful antics and welcomed affection even in the middle of the night when they wake us up. I thank Frisky every day for his friendship and giving me the opportunity to relate in a very different way to death.

As I think about transitions, what comes to mind are two dao yin practices. Ah-Ma-Ohm encourages us to move gracefully from the material aspect of ourselves to the spirit. Agony and Surrender acknowledges the suffering we may experience when we hold on and the freedom that comes when we finally let go.

≈ CHAPTER 30 ≈

Ah-Ma-Ohm

Unlike the other movement practices, sounds are an integral part of Ah-Ma-Ohm.

This exercise moves our attention from the belly to the head. We begin by focusing on the lower energy center, known in Chinese medicine as the lower dantian, in the lower abdomen. This area relates to our connection to the physical, earthly, material realm. Then, we move our attention to our upper abdomen and chest, what's understood as the realm of the human. Finally, we work with sound in the head, the realm of heaven. Ah-Ma-Ohm helps us explore our experience of being born into the physical world as both human and spirit.

1. Rest in a comfortable supine pose (Figures 1–3).

2. Place your hands palms down, with your fingertips touching over your navel region.

3. Inhale through your nose, focusing on bringing the breath into your belly. Notice how the belly rises up.

4. Exhale out the mouth with an "Ahhh" sound and feel the belly deflate. This sound and space relate to our experience in the womb and our transition into life outside of it.

5. Repeat two more times. Notice where you feel the vibration when you make the sound—above, around, or below the belly button.

6. Place your hands palms down, with one hand on your upper abdomen where your ribs meet your breastbone (solar plexus) and the other on your chest.

7. Inhale through your nose into both your solar plexus (upper abdomen) and chest.

8. Exhale through the mouth with the sound "Maaa." This sound and space relate to our experience of being nurtured by our mother, as well as our transition to nourishing ourselves.

9. Repeat two more times. Notice where you feel the vibration when you make the sound—in the solar plexus or chest.

10. Now, place one hand on your forehead, palm down.

11. Inhale through your nose into the space between the eyebrows.

12. Exhale through the mouth with the monotone sound "Ohm." Let the "mmm" portion be the predominant sound—at least two-thirds of the entire exhalation. Notice if you can feel the sound vibrate through your skull, brain, and body.

13. Once the exhalation and Ohm are complete, focus on the silence. This sound and space relate to our spiritual life and our connection to Universal Consciousness.

14. Repeat two more times.

15. With a single, long breath, inhale first into your belly, then into your ribs, and finally into your chest.

16. Next, exhale in three parts, being mindful of the sounds and sensations in each area. First, empty your belly with an "Ahhh" sound. Continue to exhale your chest with a "Maaa" sound. Finally, exhale between your eyebrows with an "Ohm" sound.

17. Repeat two more times.

18. Take a moment to notice how you feel from head to toe, tuning in to the presence and flow of energy in your body and the space around you.

19. Please finish with a body and breath scan.

CHAPTER 31

Agony and Surrender

Agony and Surrender is one of my favorite exercises, as it teaches us about attachment and the sweet release of letting go. This practice affects Yang Ming and the core abdominal muscles, like the psoas muscle. It benefits the back, the muscles on the top of the thighs, the shoulders, and the knees.

Agony and Surrender is best done toward the end of your practice. It is the culmination of the movements from the Shao Yang and Tai Yang systems. Notice what feelings and images emerge once you complete the sequence.

1. Begin by resting in a comfortable supine pose (Figures 1–3) and please do a body and breath scan.

2. Extend your legs straight along the mat if possible.

3. Inhale into the belly. Engage your abdominal muscles to lift your head, looking at your toes, if possible (Figure 52). If you find your neck is straining, please use your hands to help lift your head, relaxing your neck as much as possible (Figure 53).

4. Exhale and gently return your head to the mat.

5. Repeat two more times.

6. Bend your hips and knees to stand your feet, and cross your left leg over your right, with the thighs touching (Figure 17). This is your starting position.

7. Cross your arms in the opposite orientation to your legs— your right arm crosses over your left; each hand rests on the opposite shoulder if possible.

8. Inhale into the belly as you engage your abdominal muscles to lift your crossed legs toward your chest. Notice if you feel the muscles of your right leg tightening.

9. Exhale and relax to the starting position with your right foot standing on the mat.

10. Repeat two more times.

11. Inhale into the belly as you engage your abdominal muscles to lift your upper body (chest and head) toward the thighs as your right foot remains on the mat.

12. Repeat two more times.

13. Inhale into the belly as you engage your abdominal muscles to lift your knees toward your chest and your chest toward your knees, as if you were doing a crunch (Figure 63).

14. Exhale and return to the starting position. Your arms remain crossed.

15. Repeat two more times.

16. Inhale into the belly as you engage your abdominal muscles to lift your knees toward your chest and your chest toward your knees, as if you were doing a crunch. This time hold the breath in and tighten the muscles in your limbs and face while in the crunch (Figure 64).

17. Hold your breath as you gently return your body to the mat.

18. Exhale and relax as your arms and legs remain crossed, with your right foot standing on the mat.

19. Repeat two more times.

20. Inhale into the belly as you engage your abdominal muscles to lift your chest to your knees and your knees to your chest. Hold your breath and tighten the muscles of your entire body. Gently release just your head away from your chest, though it won't come to rest on the mat (Figure 65).

21. As you continue holding your breath with your arms and legs crossed, gently return your body to the mat.

22. Exhale and relax as your arms and legs remain crossed, with your right foot standing on the mat.

23. Repeat two more times.

24. Return to a comfortable supine pose (Figures 1–3). Please do a body and breath scan. Do you notice any areas that feel heavier or longer than others? Notice if any areas feel tense or relaxed. What else do you notice, if anything?

25. Repeat the entire practice with the arms and legs crossed the opposite way.

Figure 63

Figure 64

Figure 65

CHAPTER 32

Vortex and Splash

Almost daily, I visit my neighborhood river or one of the many creeks that feed into it. I practice putting my attention into the way the water moves—how it twists and turns, jumps and splashes, ultimately coming to rest back into itself, deep and still. I learned this way of appreciating water's flow through an extraordinary person whose mission is to protect and conserve water.

Back when I was studying in Chengdu, Dave, my friend and internship partner, and I would occasionally go to brunch at the Jinjiang Hotel. Catering to Westerners, the hotel served familiar foods like omelets, bacon, and croissants in an upscale, contemporary atmosphere. More than just the comfort food and luxurious indoor heating, we sought refuge in relationships with other English speakers. We'd listen in on conversations and when the eavesdropping proved interesting, introduce ourselves.

One lucky day, we met Betsy Damon, the founder and director of Keepers of the Water. As we brunched together, we learned that through her environmental education nonprofit, Betsy engaged communities, students, scientists, and artists in projects that heighten awareness of the quality, sustainability, and regeneration of water. Part of her passion was making sure people had access to clean water. She had been invited to Chengdu by the Chinese government to design and build the country's first inner-city ecological water park, the Living Water Garden.

As a former environmental ecologist and now a healthcare

practitioner, I was particularly enthusiastic about her project. The Living Water Garden would engage people to witness nature's ability to heal itself and teach residents about the possibility of restoring clean water. I imagined it might also awaken in visitors the realization of their own potential for self-healing, given the right circumstances. When we met, Betsy was laying the groundwork for the six-acre park. Her vision involved diverting water from the putrid Fu-Nan River that runs through the populous city and channeling it through a human-made riverbed that included a wetland, settling pond, and series of fish and plant ponds. This process would transform the polluted water into potable water.

An artist as well as activist, Betsy was designing sculptures she called "flow forms," a critical feature of the park's riverbed that would create a vortex motion in the water much like rocks in a river. Her work was based on the science that shows how water, when moving along a stream or riverbed over a distance, gets aerated and cleansed.

Betsy was as interested in us and our study of Chinese medicine as we were in her work. That mutual curiosity and appreciation led to her extending an invitation to join her on her field trips researching streams and rivers in Western China. Having spent years living and doing research in aquatic environments, I was all in.

One of my favorite outings was our exploration of the creek that runs through the Wolong National Nature Reserve in the Qionglai Mountains region of Sichuan. As we made our way over and around the creek's boulders, we stopped frequently to observe how the water flowed and spiraled. The roaring, bubbling water so charged the air that even the hair on my arms stood to attention as we boulder-hopped our way up the creek. Here and there, the water slowed into deep, crystal-clear, turquoise pools that beckoned us to regroup and rest.

While we wandered, Betsy sketched the position and shape of the rocks, as well as the patterns the water made as it tumbled and pooled. From her sketches, she created designs for flow form sculptures that would recreate the movement patterns she observed in nature. She then took her designs to a sculptor in Chengdu who carved or cast them in granite or cement. The flow form sculptures would be placed along the park's riverbed, creating a variety of circulation pathways and mini waterfalls. Thanks to the experience of observing water with Betsy, I gained a fresh appreciation and curiosity for its spiraling movement and how it can purify itself by the nature of that movement.

Our individual purification is similar. In fact, self-transformation through movement is a key theme in dao yin. After checking in with myself through a body scan, I begin my personal practice and most dao yin classes with a twist. A playful movement, twists are easy to do and can be so satisfying. I feel refreshed mentally and physically just from a few simple twists. I've also noticed how often students will engage in a twist, quite spontaneously, after doing a challenging movement. Like animals that shake vigorously after a stressful or exciting encounter, we use twists as a reset.

Just like the water flowing through Betsy's flow forms in the Living Water Garden, twisting is essential to our health and transformation. When I think about the primal movement of rolling from our backs onto our bellies as babes, to the spiral arrangement of tissues in our heart and blood vessels, it's evident to me that twists and spirals play an essential role in our survival and development. As I've rolled through my own life, many of the choices I've made have been a result of weighing the consequences of what could happen as a result of going this way or that, right or left. Turning toward and away from options, weighing the pros and cons, is how I ultimately decide which direction to go.

Your journey may be much like mine, full of twists and turns. My life's flow has involved repeatedly turning toward or away from situations and choices that didn't serve me well. Now, I don't regret the choices that led me down drama-filled or difficult paths. Though I chided myself for repeatedly making the same detrimental choices, they were, in truth, important opportunities for building awareness, getting feedback, learning, distilling the essence of my values, growing, and evolving.

Let's check out the results of twisting with a powerful practice for detoxification: Sidewinder.

CHAPTER 33

Sidewinder

Sidewinder works the side body and benefits the shoulders and hips. This practice resonates with the Shao Yang channel system and is about consolidating energy into the waist where we tend to accumulate body fat. I think of it as being like sweeping dust into a pile to more easily dispose of it. Gathering up energy into a specific area helps the body have a more thorough release. When you come to your body and breath scan after this pressure-building practice, check in with your chest, lungs, ribs, and abdomen. Notice if you feel a sense of release or expansion in any of these areas. Sidewinder can improve your digestion, as it benefits the gallbladder.

1. Please come to rest in a supine position (Figures 1–3) and do a body and breath scan.

2. Come to rest in a right side-lying position (Figures 7–8).

3. Feel the weight of the left knee and lower leg on your right knee and lower leg.

4. With your knees together, inhale and lift your left lower leg, from the knee down, off the right (Figure 66). Notice if you feel any pressure or sensation in belly, ribs, hips, buttocks, legs, or anywhere else.

5. Exhale and relax back to the starting position.

6. Repeat two more times.

7. This time, inhale as you lift both your right and left lower legs off the mat (Figure 67). Keep your legs touching as best you can. If you experience pain while lifting both legs, lift only your top shin/ankle/foot and leave your lower leg resting on the ground.

8. Repeat two more times.

9. Exhale and relax back to the starting position.

10. Next, lift your left arm over the side of your head and place your left palm over the right ear. Your left elbow should be just above the crown of your skull. Your head is resting in the palm of your left hand (Figure 68).

11. Inhale. Using your left arm and hand, gently raise your head, as if to make the letter "C." Your left side will be folding as your right side lengthens (Figure 69). Notice if you feel sensations anywhere along the entire length of your left or right side.

12. Repeat two more times.

13. Exhale and relax back to the starting position.

14. Now, as you inhale, lift your upper body off the floor. At the same time, while keeping your knees together, lift both lower legs off the floor (Figure 70). Remember, if you cannot lift both lower legs, then lift just the left lower leg.

15. Exhale and relax back to the starting position.

16. Repeat two more times.

17. Rest in supine position (Figures 1–3) and do a body and breath scan.

18. Notice how the left side you've just worked feels compared to the right. Notice the leg length and weight, as well as any sensations in the ribs, chest, and lungs.

19. Repeat the entire sequence while lying on your left side.

20. During your closing body and breath scan, notice any sensation along the sides of your body, from your armpits through your waist and hips to the sides of your legs.

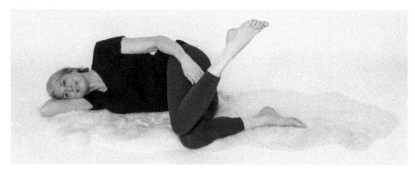

Figure 66

Figure 67

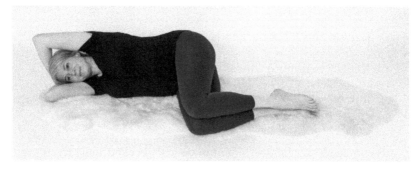

Figure 68

Figure 69

Figure 70

CHAPTER 34

Reishi and the Hermit

After completing my Asian medicine training and returning to North Carolina, I reached out to acupuncturists in Western North Carolina, seeking colleagues and resources. As a new practitioner, I knew I'd need to create a community of support for clinical case review. I also wanted to find someone who was as passionate as I about herbal medicine.

As luck would have it, I met an excellent practitioner, among the first Chinese medicine practitioners to graduate in the United States, who took me under his wing at his clinic in Asheville. There, I worked one day a week dispensing herbs to patients. Through camaraderie, banter, and serious conversation, I learned important skills from Phil in managing an herbal medicine pharmacy, the patient–practitioner relationship, diagnosis, and treatment.

My fortune continued to grow, as just down the road from my home and practice was Joe Hollis, an internationally recognized horticulturalist and herbal medicine grower. He was also the founder of Mountain Gardens, home to the largest collection of organically grown, native Appalachian and Chinese medicinal herbs in the Eastern United States. An enthusiast of Chinese philosophy and medicine, Joe maintained a pharmacy of Chinese herbs, many of which he learned to cultivate here. Wanting to continue my studies in herbal medicine, I naturally turned to him.

The seeds of our friendship were sown over cups of tea. When the weather was good, we'd sit and sip on the porch overlooking the garden. When it got colder, we'd stoke the wood fire and bundle up in his mountain log cabin. Our conversations encompassed herbal medicine and readings from the Chinese medicine classics. We quietly delighted in our mutual interests.

As much as I wanted to connect with him and learn everything I could, I recognized Joe as a fellow introvert. Not wanting to impose, I approached our friendship with patience, grateful for whatever he chose to impart. In time, I felt confident enough in our rapport to ask him to be my apothecary. He enthusiastically accepted.

Not only has Joe served as my apothecary for all these years, he's also been a treasured friend. When my son Paolo showed an interest in studying with him, Joe graciously took him on as an intern.

Reishi (also known as Ling Zhi or Ganoderma mushroom) was one of the Chinese herbs Joe taught Paolo how to find, harvest, and prepare as medicine. Paolo, in turn, taught me.

Our first reishi-finding foray took us to the woods behind our home. Reishi seem to know how to be just out of sight. However, Paolo told me if I were willing to walk around the base of a declining or nearly dead hemlock, I'd most likely be rewarded. We were. That little adventure reignited my passion for harvesting wild medicinal herbs, something I hadn't done in years.

My favorite place to visit and harvest reishi is high up on the Black Mountains, along a rushing creek. Here, tall Carolina hemlocks, most of which are in decline, dot the creek bank.

What delights me about the mushroom is how its appearance tells us what it does for us. Its kidney shape and ripply surface, reminiscent of the ripples in the creek, tell us it is good for our kidneys. Held sideways, it looks like an ear. Here, the law of signatures lets us know reishi may also benefit our hearing. The mushroom's crimson-maroon color indicates it benefits the heart. "The mushroom of immortality," as reishi is nicknamed, is treasured by Daoists for promoting a long and healthy life, and by herbalists as an adaptogen and immune modulator.

In my years of working with Joe and other healers, I've learned to be reverent when harvesting herbs. After all, we are calling on nature to support our lives. As I pick and use herbs as medicine or food, I'm mindful to contemplate the miracle of nature, our place in it, and our interdependence.

I savor my reishi-picking experiences, which feel like a pilgrimage. Even though I intend to gather only a few mushrooms, I spend a full day between hiking the trail, stopping to look up at the forest canopy, and visiting one of several waterfalls before reaching the "Mother Tree." This tall hemlock has so many small and large reishi growing on one side that they look like an apron wrapping the tree's hips.

Once at the Mother Tree, I rest. Thanks to several herbal medicine mentors, I think to ask the tree how many mushrooms I might take and listen within to arrive at a number. This time, it's six mushrooms. I pluck a hair from my head and offer it to the tree, another lesson I learned from a Native American friend, to signal gratitude for nature's gift. I listen to the water and the quiet squeak of my blade against the mushrooms' flesh. I spend a few minutes admiring their color, sheen, and shape, and place them gently in my basket. Before parting, I hug the tree, which is so large my arms reach only halfway around. I return to the creek and appreciate how it nourishes the tree and the mushrooms. Finally, I give thanks to Joe and Paolo for their inspiration.

I'm reminded of a beautiful silk scarf that Joe once gave me as a way to thank me for sharing this journey of plant medicine with him. The print on the scarf was not what most people would think of as beautiful: in the center of the smooth ivory silk was an image of reishi mushrooms. I felt he had bestowed a great honor upon me.

I don't have a scarf to honor you for sharing this journey with me, but I do have the final dao yin practice, the one that makes me think of Joe. I thank him for teaching me how to take care of myself and others through this medicine, and how to care for our natural world as we do our work. May this self-massage practice be the hug you give yourself to honor yourself for taking the time to pay attention, move, explore, and rest as you cultivate your understanding of who you truly are.

CHAPTER 35

Circulate and Harmonize Self-Massage

Building and circulating our energy are the ultimate benefits of dao yin practice. Once the energy is moving, we want to make sure it gets evenly distributed throughout the body. A simple head-to-toe self-massage is an ideal method for distributing the energy. It relaxes our tissues, stimulates acupuncture points and meridians to improve organ function, and grounds and settles our energy. This self-massage, characterized by pushing and rubbing down your body with your hands, is an integral part of dao yin practice. Unless otherwise noted, your breathing can be slow, long, and deep, or however feels natural to you. Repeat each massage three or nine times.

1. Sitting comfortably, rub your palms together with enough pressure and speed to generate heat in them.

2. Gently tap your entire scalp with your fingertips, starting at the crown of the head and working your way throughout the scalp.

3. Place your right palm on your forehead, fingers extended and pointing to the left. Lightly stroke your fingers against your face, starting between the eyebrows (Yin Tang point), and move down over the nose and upper lip (Du 26) to the tip of your chin.

4. Repeat with your left hand. Continue alternating hands for a total of three or nine strokes.

5. With your index fingers extended and the rest of your fingers folded into your palms, gently stroke with your index fingertips from the outer edge of your nostrils upward to the inner corner of your eyes (Large Intestine 20 to Bladder 1). Repeat for a total of three or nine times.

6. Extend your index and middle fingers together while curling the rest of your fingers into your palms. Place the tips of your extended fingers on your temples and rub your temple region as you circle either clockwise or counterclockwise three or nine times.

7. Place the tips of your thumbs onto your temples with the rest of your fingers pointing upward, palms forward. Bend your index fingers into a hook shape and curl all the other fingertips into your palms. Place the knuckles of your hook-shaped index fingers on the inner eyebrows, just above your nose. Exhale as you gently stroke your index finger knuckles from the inside to the outside edge of your eyebrows. From here, inhale as you move in a circular pattern under your eye, along your cheekbone, toward the bridge of your nose, and up again to your inner eyebrow point. Repeat for a total of three or nine times.

8. Use the tips of your index fingers to stroke from the inner corner of your eyes, down along the contours of your cheeks, along the lower border of your cheekbone as you exhale. Inhale as you stroke back up to the outer edges of your eyes. Repeat for a total of three or nine times.

9. Make a peace sign with both of your hands and place your middle finger in front of your ear and your index finger behind it. Maintaining the peace-sign distance between your index

and middle fingers, exhale as you gently stroke downward along your jaw to your chin. Repeat for a total of three or nine times.

10. Extend your index fingers and curl the other fingers into your palms. Center one index finger above your upper lip and the other below your lower lip. Exhale as you slide your fingers outward, as wide as the corners of your mouth, and then inhale as you slide them back, pressing in both directions. Repeat for a total of three or nine times.

11. Place your right palm on the left side of your throat, behind your side neck muscles. Stroke downward from behind your right ear, along the side of your neck to your right collarbone. Repeat this motion with your left hand against the right side of your neck. That's one neck massage. Repeat on the left and right sides, alternating, for a total of three or nine times. Please be sure *not* to press on both sides of your neck at the same time.

12. Place your palms on your upper back where your neck meets your back. Exhale as you slide your hands toward your collarbones as you simultaneously drop your head backward. Repeat for a total of three or nine swipes.

13. Place your right palm on your left shoulder, with your left palm cupping your right elbow. Massage your shoulder and elbow nine times in a circular motion. Switch sides and repeat for a total of nine times.

14. Extend your right arm in front of you with your right palm facing up. Place your left palm on your right shoulder. Exhale as you slide your left palm down the right arm to the right palm. Turn your right palm down, placing your left palm on the back of your right hand. Inhale as you slide your left palm up from your right hand to your right shoulder. Repeat for

a total of three or nine times. Switch sides and repeat for a total of three or nine times.

15. Place your right hand on your upper right chest and your left hand on your left upper chest. Slide your right hand down on a diagonal over the chest and breastbone, in a diving motion, toward your left belly and hip. Then slide your left hand, in a diving motion, diagonally down to your right hip. Alternate sides, three or nine times.

16. Interlace your fingers, place the palms of your hands over your navel, and massage your navel, moving clockwise three or nine times and then counterclockwise for the same number of repetitions. Envision 12 o'clock at the sternum and 6 o'clock at the pubic bone.

    Please stand up with feet parallel and shoulder-width apart. Your knees are slightly bent. Let your tailbone drop, inviting your spine to lengthen.

17. Place the backs of your hands on your low back, just above your hip bones and below your ribs. This is the kidney area. Rub your kidneys in a circular motion nine times, either clockwise or counterclockwise.

18. With your hands in the same location as the previous exercise, inhale and slide the backs of your hands as high up as you comfortably can. Exhale and rub down your back on each side. Massage both sides at the same time. Repeat this massage for a total of three or nine times.

19. Place your palms on the sides of your hips. Exhale and rub downward along the outsides of your legs to your ankles, bending forward as far as you comfortably can from your hips. From this forward bend position, inhale and rub up the insides of your legs, returning to standing with your hands on your hips. Repeat for a total of three or nine times.

20. Bend your knees. With the palms of your hands, exhale as you pat the backs of your legs from your buttocks to your heels. Pat up the insides of the legs as you inhale to return to standing. Repeat for a total of three or nine times.

21. Widen your stance so your feet are shoulder-width apart. Twist to the left from your waist, allowing your arms to swing. As you reach the fullness of the twist, tap your left shoulder with the palm of your right hand as you simultaneously tap/pat your right kidney area with the back of your left hand. Swing to the right, letting the back of your right hand tap your left kidney area while your left palm taps your right shoulder. Twist in this way three or nine times.

22. Twist to the left from your waist, allowing your arms to swing. As you reach the fullness of the twist, tap your left lower belly with the palm of your right hand, as you simultaneously tap/pat your right kidney area with the back of your left hand. Swing to the right, letting the back of your right hand tap your left kidney area and your left palm tap your right lower belly. Twist in this way three or nine times.

23. Cover each ear with the heel of your palms, allowing your fingertips to meet at base of your skull. Cross your index fingers over your middle fingers. As you press your index fingers on your middle fingers, simultaneously snap them downwards across the top of your middle fingers to strike the back of your skull/neck. This will sound like a drumbeat. Repeat for a total of three or nine times.

While we've now completed a dao yin practice and self-massage, there's one final movement that will help you seal in and integrate the benefits.

Stand with your feet together and your knees slightly bent. Allow your tailbone to drop and sink as if a weight were gently hanging from it toward the earth. As you ground yourself in this way, let your attention come to the spine, imagining a silken thread connecting from the crown of your head to the sky, lifting you. Notice if intentional counter forces of dropping and lifting invite your spine to effortlessly elongate.

Place your palms on your belly. Touching your thumb tips together over your belly button, let your index fingertips come to touch, creating a triangle with your hands. The other fingers can rest alongside each other, pointing downward toward the pubic bone. Your pinky fingers naturally come to rest on an acupuncture point just above the pubic bone. This point, Stomach 30 or Qi Thoroughfare, is recognized in acupuncture for helping us feel nourished by food and drink, and whatever else we digest and assimilate, including the effects of our movement practice. It helps unblock energy in the abdomen and supports circulation between the abdomen and the legs.

If you are comfortable, close your eyes until just a sliver of light is visible, gazing at the tip of your nose, or simply close your eyes. Take long deep breaths into your belly, just behind your hands. In Chinese medicine, this space is known as the lower dantian or Lower Elixir Field and believed to be the source of our energy—our battery, so to speak. If you can, imagine this energy source as a ball of light shining inside this space. As you inhale, imagine the ball of light expanding. As you exhale, imagine the ball of light condensing, becoming even brighter, gently energizing you. Your body is being filled with light. Relax as you focus on this image for several breaths.

When you feel complete, gently inhale and slowly open your eyes. Notice the feeling of your feet on the ground. Tune in to your body as you begin to look around you, taking in your environment. If possible, simultaneously be aware of your body and the space around you. Smile to yourself and the world around you. Thank yourself for taking this time and making this commitment to tune in and explore, to get to know yourself better, and to connect with the world around you.

THE WATERWAYS

CHAPTER 36

Introduction to Dao Yin Practice

Though the movements in this book may be new to you, you may discover, as you read the essential elements of these therapeutic movements, you've practiced dao yin without ever knowing it. These therapeutic exercises integrate energy (the breath), mind (attention), and body (postures and movements). Combining breathing, mindful attention, and movement fosters and develops our energy. Qigong/dao yin[1] is one of the most commonly prescribed self-care practices in Chinese medicine. It is used to treat disease, promote fitness, maintain health, and cultivate spirituality. Tai ji quan, also seen spelled as "tai chi," is a form of qigong. Yoga, which comes from India and is a therapy used in Ayurvedic medicine, also emphasizes the basic components of qigong.

While the first three reasons to practice qigong are cornerstones of many medical traditions, the last one, cultivating spirituality, is typically overlooked in contemporary Western medicine. Chinese medicine recognizes that many of our physical and mental illnesses are intertwined with our emotional, mental, and spiritual wellbeing. I believe this is a key reason why millions of Westerners who are suffering from conditions such as depression or anxiety,

---

1   Prior to being named qigong, cultivating energy through mindful movement in China was known as dao yin. Qigong is a relatively modern term, first coined in the 20th century.

or who are simply seeking to enhance their wellbeing and joy of living, turn to Asian medicine.

As a neurolinguistic programming practitioner, one of the things I appreciate most about Chinese medicine is how it uses metaphor to explain its theories and perspectives. To help you understand the significance of mindful movement, I want to take you on a journey that explores the metaphors associated with dao yin. For example, as I discovered through my teacher, one way of writing the *qi* part of the character for qigong is to use two pictograms (an image that illustrates a concept or object). The first, *wu*, a drawing that represents emptiness, everything, and nothing, implies "to start from scratch." The other, *huo*, is the symbol for a flame, heat, or fire relating to the fire of desire. When I look at these two pictograms, I am reminded we are all starting from scratch and our desire to interact and relate is what keeps us moving forward and engaging in life. It's like the physics concept of inertia that states an object at rest stays at rest until it's acted upon. Our energy is like that object. It takes desire or intention to initiate and do something with our energy.

Gong of qigong translates as putting forth effort with skill or merit. When combined, it's easy to see qigong is the practice of skillfully and mindfully cultivating our energy.

Personally, as I've cultivated my energy over all these years of practice, my relationships to myself, others, and my environment have all changed, gradually but dramatically. I've also witnessed how it helps patients and students improve their relationships with themselves and others.

Just like qigong, dao yin has a world of meaning encoded in its characters. The first, *dao*, contains the character Dao, the same Dao that is central to the philosophy of Daoism. Dao translates as "the Way of the Cosmos." The cosmos is understood to be a harmonious and orderly system governed by natural law. Daoism recognizes a relationship between nature and human beings. In essence, the practice guides us to connect with, and live in harmony with, ourselves and nature. By doing so, we return to the Dao.

Daoism is also known as the philosophy of mastering the waterways. It speaks to following in the path of the virtues of water, hence the title of my book. When we live by those virtues, we live in harmony with the Dao. In what is considered a foundational text on Daoist philosophy, the *Dao De Jing* offers that virtue is like a deep spring. Spring water bubbles up from the depths of earth and arrives on the surface pure. Without effort, this pure water extends itself, braiding together with other streams of spring water, forming creeks and rivers, filling estuaries. Ultimately, that spring water reaches the oceans. Along its long course from spring to ocean, water carves out the shape of the landscape.

Our individual experiences, as well as the way we live our lives through our thoughts, behaviors, movements, and speech, influence our physical shape in the same manner as flowing spring water carves the shape of its landscape. From our postures to our wrinkles, the shape of our body tells the story of our ancestors (our genetics), our past experiences, the accumulation of our perceptions and reactions, and our present state of mind. I have come to trust the body. I believe, though some of its responses can be misinterpreted and seem misleading, it never lies. The more I learn to pay attention, the more I can listen to and understand the story it tells and discover what I can do to influence the mind-body narrative.

Dao yin helps us change that narrative through attention to movement and awareness. Within the character *dao* of dao yin are pictograms for the eye, self, and head (also translated as "beginning") and a character that means understanding, guiding, or leading. As such, *dao* speaks of looking into, reflecting, and coming to an understanding of oneself. According to the *Dao De Jing*, we need only to understand ourselves to understand our world. Truly knowing oneself requires looking inward. I can say from experience that many new opportunities have been created as a result of tuning in. Those opportunities, in turn, have helped me see myself from a different perspective, allowing me to stretch and grow even more.

The final piece to the *dao* of dao yin is the character depicting a unit of measurement, the *cun*, or Chinese inch. *Cun* speaks to a sense of measuring oneself. The metaphor here is significant. When we stretch ourselves, we are literally exploring the measure of ourselves. *Cun* also refers to the body's major bony structures, which includes the skull, shoulder girdle, and pelvis. These structures have changed shape and size as we evolved from primates on all fours to bipedal, upright humans. In other words, *cun* calls our attention to our own evolution and growth.

Yin of dao yin is composed of the symbols for a bow and arrow. Think of it as pulling and stretching our bodies as if drawing a bow, illustrating our potential for action. Once let loose, the arrow sails forward. If we literally aim to know ourselves, practice will help direct us there. Since the practice of dao yin helps us be like water, it's interesting to note that *yin* is also the character used when speaking of diverting and directing water.

The combination of the two characters, *dao* and *yin*, invites us to mindfully stretch and move the body not only as a way of understanding and measuring ourselves, but also as a means for moving forward in our respective lives.

Mindful movement practices like dao yin emphasize the importance of building a relationship with ourselves. Through repeated practice and with attention, we become more aware of our perceptions, our limitations, and our innate ability to go beyond them. The cumulative effect of connecting and relating to ourselves results in a shift in how we connect and relate to others and our world.

THE SIGNIFICANCE OF LYING DOWN

All of the dao yin exercises described in this book are practiced lying down. Because I encourage my students to cultivate and work from the foundation of beginner's mind and this is an introductory text on dao yin, there's no better position to start in than the one we used as babies when we didn't have the ability to move beyond resting on our bellies or backs.

If you've ever observed a baby, you know they do a lot of wiggling. This side-to-side motion of the spine helps them develop the physical ability to roll over. The ability to turn onto our bellies opens up a new world of possibilities. Over a short period of time, we can support our weight on our forearms and hands, and are then able to lift our heads to see what is in front of and around us. We can interact with the world by orienting our head and hands toward the objects of our desire. From this prone position, we can begin lengthening one side of our body while shortening the other to draw up a knee toward an elbow or hand. As we begin to sense something we want to move toward or away from, we begin to crawl. We now have a little more agency in our survival and can interact with intention.

Additionally, the lying-down position is associated with our reptilian brain located toward the back of our skulls. This is the most primitive part of the brain. It governs basic functions necessary to sustain life, such as involuntary responses to stimuli like reflexes, muscle control, balance, breathing, heartbeat, feeding/digestion, and reproduction.

While lying down engages this primitive, instinctual part of our brain, the practice of dao yin brings our attention to the unconscious and spontaneous way we move. When we integrate something that is instinctual or habitual with our conscious awareness, we have agency to change and evolve.

Not taking the time to reflect on what truly nurtures and sustains us is typical for most adults. Dao yin gives us an opportunity to return to that baby-like state where we can investigate our basic needs. From here, we can develop the skills and resources to meet them. We also have the opportunity to look at what, if anything, keeps us from taking care of ourselves.

I often say to my dao yin students, "People, this ain't about just wiggling around on the floor." This is about cultivating our awareness so we can continue growing, learning to live our essence and purpose.

Another key reason these exercises are performed in the lying-down position is their physical effect on the spine and lungs. From a structural and functional viewpoint, as you rest lying down, you'll notice gravity pulls the spine toward the ground. The ribs follow suit. The resulting spine lengthening and rib stabilization allow the diaphragm to function more efficiently, giving our lungs greater capacity to expand and take in more oxygen. In that way, we can cultivate more energy. That energy helps us get from place to place and interact with the world.

The spine, which governs whether we rest, move forward, or retreat, helps us engage with the external world. The same can be said of our lungs, which, through our very breath, give us the means to survive and interact. Through the lungs, these practices done in the lying-down position help us project our voice in the world.

ABOUT MOVEMENT IN DAO YIN

Each of us develops unique habitual movement patterns based on genetics, modeling, conditioning, instinct, and repeated practice of what we've found works most efficiently or comfortably for us. We could say that our movements are programmed. The coding reveals much about how we respond and react to our perceptions and interpretations of our experiences.

Stretching and pulling the body is much like rolling out dough. When we stretch dough in one direction, it contracts from the opposite direction. As we keep rolling it back and forth, the shape changes. The result of this interplay of opposites results in our expansion, whether energetically, mentally, emotionally, or physically. Within the act of contracting and tensing comes the possibility to expand, bringing energy to previously unexamined parts of our body. Cultivating conscious awareness through the dance of contraction and expansion leads to a new shape or entity being formed.

PRACTICING MODERATION

As you practice dao yin, please move slowly and mindfully, remembering that less is more. If a movement causes discomfort or pain, please try a smaller range of motion or less effort. If that doesn't mitigate the issue, please rest and simply imagine yourself practicing a particular movement. What muscles would you have to use? What might you feel? Imagining with all your senses goes a long way to improve your movement, flexibility, and function. This is useful, especially if you have an injury and can't do the movement.

Given the slow, mindful nature of these therapeutic exercises, they are excellent for those who are elderly, menopausal, pregnant, depleted, or in recovery from illness or injury. They are also useful for those of us who consistently work hard, overdo, and infrequently rest or relax.

Even if you love the practice, please don't overdo. We are looking to cultivate energy, not consume it. I encourage you to take your time, go easy, and contain your practice time.

A NOTE ABOUT TENSION AND HOLDING

Several movements instruct you to restrict the movement of a body part, like the head and eyes, or the breath. I look at tension as an invitation to let go. When you are asked to restrict the movement of your body or breathing, notice how that restriction affects your ability to move. You can also notice if the restriction has an effect on your mental or emotional state. Notice what happens when you release the tension. You might discover the postures that have built-in tension or restriction are the ones that yield the most noticeable release.

TAKING INVENTORY

The most revealing part of dao yin, or any self-care practice, is what happens when we take a moment to observe the effects of the practice. Because one of the goals of dao yin is to consciously track our development through movement, it's essential to begin and end dao yin practice by taking inventory of what we feel at rest through a body and breath scan.

While there are many ways to do a scan, the one I employ most involves moving our attention gradually and slowly from our heels through the limbs and torso to the head. I invite you to pay attention to specific areas, such as the heels, tops of the feet, ankles, lower legs, and so forth. Your attention might be drawn to sensations on the surface of the skin, at the level of the muscles and organs, or deeper in at the level of the bones. As you notice any specific sensations in a particular area, label them with words like neutral, ache, tight, sharp, warm, cold, tingle. For example, I notice a warm tingle in the palms of my hands. This noticing and naming engages the two hemispheres of the brain, helping us to integrate our experience. Notice, too, the landscape of your body as you move your mind through it—where does your body come into contact with the ground, where does it rise up?

You can also take a more global approach to a body scan, noticing what sensations or locations call your attention. For example, as you tune in for the body scan, you might immediately notice a tightness in your right shoulder blade or a softness in your belly. You can just let your attention be drawn where your body calls it.

As you begin moving, notice your tendencies. Do you like to start out with big movements or do you prefer to start small? Do you prefer to move or breathe quickly or slowly? If you like to move quickly, what do you notice, if anything, when you slow down the breath and the movements? You are welcome to experiment.

I encourage you to do a scan at the end of an exercise. Notice if one side or part of your body feels heavier than the rest. Perhaps one side rests more clearly on the ground, or you feel your body is turned more toward one side than the other. The reason for this may be because that's the side that did most of the work. Breaking this down even more, notice whether the side you feel heaviest on or have turned toward is your dominant or non-dominant side. Through my training and personal observation, if it is on the side of your non-dominant hand, it may be a sign you are accomplishing the movement through your will, rather than your strengths. Perhaps, too, you may be compromising something in your life that doesn't quite suit you. This is a thought worth exploring. If so, you might consider what you truly want, and the resources and support you need to make it happen.

By noticing our body's response to the practices, we can become more attuned to our responses to other activities, responses we typically have without thinking. For example, many of my students tell me, having done dao yin, they are better able to notice their thoughts and emotions, and moderate their reactions to them. The more you reflect, the more your self-awareness grows, ultimately allowing you to become the master of your mind rather than the slave to it. Thoughts that in the past would have remained unnoticed are now detectable. You may notice the pause between the thought and your reaction to it starts to lengthen. There's freedom in that pause. No longer is your only choice to react involuntarily or habitually to your experience. Instead, you can choose to respond consciously to your thoughts, perceptions, environment, and sensations.

If you notice your mind wandering during a dao yin movement or the body and breath scan, give yourself a pat on the back. You just became aware of wandering attention, which typically goes unnoticed. When you notice this, gently direct your attention back to your body.

I can say from experience that directing our attention to the body and noticing sensations and responses is not always comfortable. The body can be a storehouse of tension, emotion, memories, trauma, and challenges. Sometimes, what you notice can be physically or emotionally painful. Sometimes, you might avoid paying attention to yourself to avoid discomfort. After all, you may not yet have the resources or skills to attend to or resolve the issue. It's important to give yourself the opportunity to pay attention, at whatever intensity or duration suits you best in the moment. That may change day to day, practice to practice, body scan to body scan. I encourage you to bring compassion and curiosity to what you notice. Over time, you might discover that giving yourself this attention is like arriving at your own personal oasis.

One way to become more at ease with whatever you feel is to ask yourself a few simple questions. If you notice a sensation, ask yourself if that sensation has a shape or size, a color or sound. Relating your physical experience using descriptive words, such as soft, big, round, peach-colored, and quiet, can take some of the pressure off. You can also ask the question, "And this sensation is like what?" You might get a juicy metaphor here, which will give you a way to look at whatever you are experiencing from a different perspective to gain more insight.

BREATHING

Inhale and exhale through the nose, unless you are not well, in which case exhale out of the mouth. Please note, exhaling through the mouth is required for some of the movements. This is to ensure a full release.

Breathing can help us move with greater ease and efficiency. When you are asked to hold the breath while moving, notice how that affects the movement. What happens when you release the held breath? When the instructions invite you to breathe freely, allow the movements to partner with the breath.

SPEED

While you are getting used to this practice, I encourage you to move slowly. Moving slowly helps you maintain your attention, allowing your mind and body to work together. This slow tempo is also recommended for the breath. I've noticed some of my students prefer to go quickly through the movements. Typically, this is a habitual response, so I remind them they might discover gems if they give themselves ample time for exploration. It's important not to cheat yourself of this essential integration of mind and body. If you are curious about experiencing the movement quickly, please do, in as mindful a manner as possible.

REPETITION

Repetition also plays a role in cultivating our awareness. Most of the movements are repeated three times. The number three and its multiples are significant in Daoism, where three is the bridge between the divine and the mundane. Beyond these esoteric notions, three repetitions give us time to let the movement soak in, kind of like reading a poem or listening to a symphonic movement a few times to let its meaning and essence sink in. Another way to look at repetition of movement is that it nags us to pay attention and become aware of ourselves. Repetition drives home the importance of attending to ourselves through self-reflection and self-maintenance.

THE POTENCY OF THE EYES

Dao yin is about taking our attention inward; if you notice your eyes wanting to close, let them. This is both appropriate and helpful. Please note, some of the exercises ask that you have your eyes open and focused in a particular way.

TIMING

You can practice dao yin daily. It's recommended to practice for 20 minutes at the same time, in the same space. Some practitioners go so far as to do the practice wearing an outfit dedicated to dao yin. Daily practice is optimal but do what you can. The best times are in the morning or evening when we are at ease and able to lie down.

Lying on your firm bed or on the bedroom floor as you prepare for sleep is especially delightful. This is also a time when the stomach is empty and not digesting food, another recommendation for practice.

SEQUENCING

In general, I recommend sequencing the practices in one of two ways.

One way is to start with movements that engage the lower body. Follow those with exercises that involve moving your chest, and end with movements that focus on or require working your neck and head.

Another way to sequence the movements is to start with Shao Yang practices, which involve twisting or side bending. Think of this as wanting to grease the hinges on the door before asking your body to move from outdoors to indoors and vice versa. After you work Shao Yang, work Tai Yang and finally Yang Ming.

CURIOSITY AND SENSITIVITY

When you feel ready to begin practicing the movements, I encourage you to ask yourself some questions:

- What sensations do I notice, if any?

- What kinds of sensations are they?

- Whereabouts are those sensations?

- What muscles or limbs are doing most of the work?

- Am I aware of areas that feel relaxed or tight?

- Is there a way for me to be relaxed even while I am executing a movement?

- Can I complete a movement effortlessly?

As you investigate, you'll start to notice things about your body and breathing of which you were not previously conscious.

As you become more sensitive to your body and breath, you can become more conscious of the typically unconscious movements, such as how you roll over or how you come to standing. There is potential here for you not only to have greater conscious agency over your movements and how you use your body, but also cultivate the potential to shift your physiology. If you've ever seen documentation of Tibetan monks raising their body temperature or altering their heart rate and blood pressure, it is not magic. It is because of their agency through conscious awareness over these autonomic processes.

COME BACK TO AWARENESS

As tuning inward becomes easier, you might notice that you can shift your attention off specific sensations or areas of the body and onto awareness itself. You might experience the activity of your mind—your thoughts and emotions—as something that is happening on the sidelines, something with which you don't need to get involved. Here you might meet a moment of profound stillness and silence. Notice your response to that stillness.

A FINAL NOTE

When dao yin movements come from that space of awareness, they are a spontaneous response, the result of looking within oneself rather than at one's reflection in a mirror or an outside instructor. As such, they cannot be mimicked or mirrored.

After practicing the movements according to the specific instructions I offer here, you may find your body wants to do something other than follow the guidelines.

Let it.

Ultimately, dao yin is about creating your own unique movements in the world based on self-reflection.

Be spontaneous. Be yourself.

CHAPTER 37

The Warp and Weft: Basic Steps for Self-Diagnosis

One of the greatest shifts I've made in my clinical practice is placing more emphasis on health education, lifestyle medicine, and prevention. This not only ensures longer-lasting benefit, but it also inspires patients to help themselves and take charge of their wellbeing.

What if you could mitigate or resolve health concerns and, at the same time, lay the groundwork for future prevention? It's easy once you realize your body is not only one of the greatest pharmacies ever created, it is also a state-of-the-art laboratory and you're its best researcher. The key is understanding how to do the research. Though the simple diagnostic tools I'm sharing will allow you to assess your symptoms and select dao yin movements to experiment with, please consult a licensed acupuncturist before beginning, as there is no substitute for professional assessment and guidance. Then, I encourage you to explore with curiosity, compassion, and attention to help you discover for yourself what movements serve you best.

Pain or discomfort may be due to a structural or functional issue, mental and emotional states, and our lifestyle or habits. Since dao yin movements address the energy and circulation that support our organs and tissues, as well as affect our state of mind, they help us address myriad causes of discomfort. Let's begin by investigating what factors set your challenges in motion or what makes them better or worse. The most common triggers or aggravators include movement, environment, food, thoughts, and stress. No matter the trigger or aggravator, you can use movement as medicine.

Here, we will focus on a particular channel grouping associated with the musculoskeletal system. First, let's have a brief overview of meridians or channels. The channels or meridians of Chinese medicine are simply avenues through which energy and blood circulate, kind of like the way a riverbed is the avenue through which water flows. There are five distinct types of channels in Chinese medicine. If you've ever gone to an acupuncturist, you might have seen a map of the human body hanging on a wall with lines and points drawn on it. That map most likely illustrated the primary meridians, channels of energy that support organ function. For our purposes, we are looking at another type of meridian, the sinew or tendinomuscular channels that support the structure or framework of our bodies.

The best place to start in diagnosis for the sinew system is to notice where the pain/discomfort is located. Check the sinew channel maps (Illustrations 1–6) to identify the sinew pathway(s) that correspond with the location of your pain. It's possible you'll find your trouble spot on more than one map. For simplicity, we are going to focus on only half of the 12 sinew channels, the six that relate to the exterior aspects of the body.[1] I have found, quite reliably, that these are the "mother" channels: if you treat these, you'll affect the other half of the sinew channels.

---

1   A note for acupuncturists: As you can see, I've discussed only three of the six divisions, focusing on the yang channels, in this abbreviated diagnostic method. What you'll find as you practice dao yin is that when we address the three external/yang divisions first, the internal/yin divisions are positively impacted. I have found this can be simplified even further to focusing initially on the leg yang sinew channels. I believe this is because the leg yang sinew channels, unlike the arm yang sinews, span the body from head to toe, covering a wide range of problem areas and functionality. For simplicity for a broad audience, here I have mentioned only the yang divisions and the yang sinew channels.

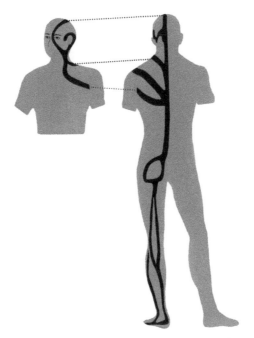

Illustration 1: Tai Yang Urinary Bladder

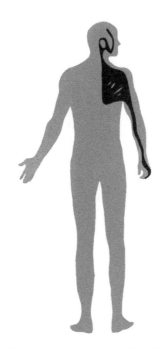

Illustration 2: Tai Yang Small Intestine

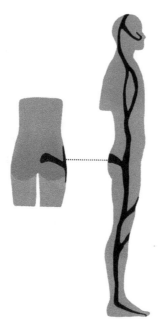

Illustration 3: Shao Yang Gall Bladder

Illustration 4: Shao Yang Triple Heater

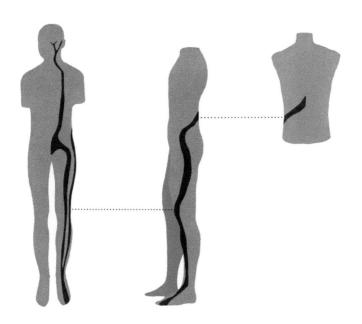

Illustration 5: Yang Ming Stomach

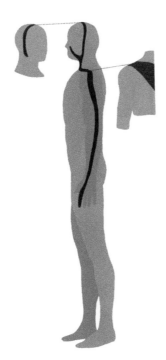

Illustration 6: Yang Ming Large Intestine

The next step is to home in on one or two channel systems by investigating the actions that alleviate or increase pain. Ask yourself these questions.

1. *Is your mobility, flexibility, or functioning hampered or worsened when you stand up from sitting, take a step forward, reach for something in front of you, or reach above your head?*

In Chinese medicine, these movements are associated with extending ourselves into the world to engage with it. For these concerns, we can explore movements that stimulate the Greater Yang (Tai Yang) channels. The Tai Yang channels relate to the small intestine and urinary bladder (Illustrations 1 and 2). These channels are found on the posterior or back side of the entire body. The back, with the bony structures of the skull, shoulder blades, spine, ribs, and sacrum, provides protection for the vital organs.

If you think about it, the back is the part of the body we show when we don't feel safe, as we defend ourselves or attack. Think of soldiers rushing toward the enemy with the back rounded and the head tucked into the chest. Tai Yang relates to how we extend into the world, further and faster, reaching out and engaging in action. When we want to engage, the spine needs to be upright, flexible, and strong, allowing the front of our body to lift and expand. This enables us to orient our senses to take in information that helps us navigate and move forward. Our ability to extend ourselves also depends on how resourced and resourceful we feel. Confidence and courage, as well as will and ambition, play an important role in being able to move forward in life. Sometimes, pain in this zone has to do with feeling afraid, over-extended, or under-resourced.

The movements in this zone involve the back and shoulder blades, and the actions of extension as in back and forward bends and reaching. I refer you to the following practices to explore Tai Yang: Locust Looks East and West, Lizard Runs Across the Water, Locust Looks Ahead, and Stretch the Bow.

2. *Does twisting your torso, turning your head, or rotating your arms or legs contribute to your discomfort? The action of twisting, turning, or rotating is associated with making choices and plans; should I go this way or that? Do you have difficulty making decisions or choices? Is there an inner conflict or uncertainty about whether to extend yourself into the world or retreat and rest? Is it time to expand yourself or contract? Are you making compromises that don't suit you?*

If twisting, turning, or rotating is your trigger or aggravator, or if one shoulder or hip is higher than the other, explore movements that relate to the Lesser Yang (Shao Yang) channels, which include the gall bladder and the triple heater (Illustrations 3 and 4). These govern the sides of the body, the sides of the head, neck, shoulders, ribs, and hips. This channel system is especially interesting as it acts as the pivot, gate, or mediator between the exterior and the interior, between Tai Yang and Yang Ming.

The energy of Shao Yang affects our ability to imagine and manifest our vision. Organizing, planning, decision making, and having the confidence to initiate and fulfill a plan are all under its purview. This level relates also to the smooth flow of energy in the body. As we relate to the world and encounter obstacles, we can move flexibly under, over, around, and through them, like a bubbling brook moves through a wood.

Shao Yang is the gatekeeper that influences extension and contraction. It's the negotiator for when to extend our energy and influence into the world or retreat and conserve our energy. Shao Yang helps us balance these two polar opposites. According to biologic principles, all life seeks homeostasis—stability, harmony, balance. This channel system is perhaps the most important one to exercise, since homeostasis is critical for survival. That's why so many of the movements in this series incorporate twisting or side bending. The Shao Yang movements Swimming Snake and Bamboo Twist are a perfect place to begin your practice. To explore further, experiment with Sidewinder, Welcome Breath, and Frog Shimmy.

3. Does sitting or lifting something trigger or intensify pain?

If so, it's possible you are asking your body to bear too much weight, or bear weight too often. This could be your own physical weight, the proverbial "weight of the world," or an object you are trying to lift or carry. It could also indicate you are doing too much in general, and not getting enough rest, nourishment, and support. Perhaps it's time to contract, retreat, and go inward. Conversely, it's also possible that this channel is speaking to you due to a lack of engagement stemming from disappointment or discouragement, as when we are literally or figuratively in a slump. In either case, you can work with movements that support your core muscles like your psoas and abdominal muscles, and your digestive system. These movements involve the Bright Yang (Yang Ming) channels, namely the stomach and large intestine, located on the front of the body (Illustrations 5 and 6). This level relates to the anterior, front part of the body. This is the region that houses our vital organs. When we feel defensive or are reluctant to engage with the world, we protect or hide this part of the body by making it concave, causing us to hold our energy within.

Conversely, when we feel nourished, safe, and supported, we are more willing to be vulnerable and engage. We open this area to enhance our capacity to connect to and embrace what we want.

The movements that correspond with this level have to do with the abdomen and chest, and the actions of bearing weight, lifting, squeezing, hugging, and holding. Explore Agony and Surrender and Returning to the Core for a hearty workout for this sinew meridian.

≈

These actions—extending, reaching, twisting, sitting, or lifting—may also help you feel better, which is important to notice. If you benefit from any of the actions described above, I encourage you to practice the dao yin movements related to that action to strengthen it. Conversely, you can practice movements related to those actions that make the pain worse. For example, if you have lower back pain that is worsened by sitting but improved by getting up and walking, or engaging in activities, practice the movements for Yang Ming (sitting) as well as Tai Yang (getting up and walking).

The best way to understand which movements will be of greatest benefit is to incorporate just one exercise at a time. Practice the movement daily for three days and note its effects. If you have no negative effects, continue with that movement, perhaps adding another to your practice. If you discover a movement practice has a negative effect, stop using that exercise. If you notice you are feeling discouraged if a movement doesn't serve you, simply choose a different exercise. You may also want to seek professional guidance from an acupuncturist, since the simple diagnostic process I've shared here may not be sufficient to address a more complex situation. Additionally, an acupuncturist can help you identify appropriate changes to your lifestyle and offer support to keep you motivated and well-resourced to make changes.

Benefits can be so subtle you might not notice them at first. If you don't notice any changes, be patient and continue. Time and practice will tell. Often, one or two weeks of daily practice will reveal those benefits.

Once you notice any improvements, which usually occur within the first few days or weeks, continue the practice less frequently. For example, if you practiced the movement daily and your pain is 50 percent better, try practicing every other day and notice if your progress continues with less practice. Continue to taper and see how your body responds. If the pain comes back, return to practice. If the pain goes away, stop practicing. See what happens. If the same symptoms recur, return to the movements.

You might notice benefits beyond your musculoskeletal system. Many patients who use the movements to treat physical pain discover that deeper, chronic issues related to organ function, skin conditions, and mental-emotional issues also improve. For example, a patient with chronic low back pain found that the Yang Ming movements also improved their symptoms from Crohn's disease and relieved anxiety they had struggled with since childhood. I recommend journaling so you can track the changes and gain insight from your experience. You might be surprised to discover how connected your movements are with many facets of your health and wellbeing.

CHAPTER 38

Case Studies

It's an honor to witness the rewarding discoveries my patients make. What surfaces as a result of practice often surprises them. In many cases, and as you'll see in these examples, the effects of practice are powerful enough that patients don't need the support of regular acupuncture treatments. It's empowering for them to realize they have the capacity within themselves and the tools to heal. When we show up for practice, bear witness to our experience, develop a deeper awareness of ourselves, and see the results of practice, we not only open ourselves to what's possible, we also expand our horizon of possibilities, many times discovering possibilities we didn't even know existed. This elicits a sense of intense optimism, as if we realize we are on the verge of what gamers refer to as an "epic win."

"If my body can heal that, what else can it heal?" This is a statement I hear frequently from patients and students as they reflect on the changes that come from practice. For those unfamiliar with Asian medicine, our health concerns stem from myriad sources including: mental, emotional, and physical issues; the food, medicine, and drink we ingest; our activities; family and personal health history; our constitution; environmental factors; the way we breathe; our thoughts, beliefs, attitudes, and ideas. When we affect one thing, we open ourselves to the possibility of affecting all things connected to it. In other words, the benefits of this medicine manifest as a ripple effect.

Discovering we have the power and potential within to positively affect our health and wellbeing through our awareness, lifestyle, and self-care is the most empowering and important discovery my patients and students make.

CASE 1

A child psychologist came to see me as part of her commitment to optimal health. For about a year, she was experiencing limited range of motion in her left arm due to stiffness and an ache in her left shoulder. She reported that sometimes the pain was sharp, making it difficult for her to reach her arm around to put on a jacket or fasten her bra. The shoulder pain referred down her triceps muscle (located at the back of the arm) and up her trapezius (a muscle along the back and sides of the neck, shoulder, and upper back region). She noted muscle weakness in the left wrist and hand.

Since her pain was worsened by rotating and extending her arm, I was interested in exploring poses that affect the Shao Yang (worse with rotating) and Tai Yang (worse with extension) channels.

To start her off simply, I offered one practice for Tai Yang, Locust Looks East and West (Chapter 20). This movement involves lifting the chest into a backbend while the head is turned to one side and arm is bent, thus activating the muscles alongside the spine and those wrapping the shoulder blades. I demonstrated the movement and then led her through the practice. She noted that she felt a difference in her freedom of movement between her left and right sides. As she placed her arm and turned her head to look at her left elbow, she felt stiffness in the left shoulder. Since it didn't cause pain, we continued working lying down. Had it felt painful to her, I would have recommended and demonstrated doing the position standing up against a wall to eliminate the pressure of the floor and weight of her body and head resting on her left arm and hand.

By her second day of practice, the patient let me know she could do the dao yin practice with less stiffness on the left side. Since her condition improved just with that one exercise for Tai Yang, there was no need to add a practice for Shao Yang.

By day four, her range of motion had improved so much, she could do the movement almost as easily on the left as she could on the right. She also shared that she could put her jacket on with greater ease. Twisting her arm/shoulder to secure her bra was no longer painful. She returned a week later, reporting she had no pain and no ache, and could sleep on her left shoulder for the first time in many months.

She remarked that of the varied bodywork therapies she had tried for her shoulder pain, she was clear this had helped the most. Satisfied with her improvement, we agreed she could continue with dao yin. I also recommended other self-care practices and invited her to come back for treatment whenever needed. Two years later, she continues dao yin, her shoulder is pain-free, and she's shared Locust Looks East and West with friends experiencing similar pain.

CASE 2

A plumber and avid amateur football player was concerned about back pain that had gone on for over six months. The pain became acute one day while he was carrying a load of supplies into a house. He felt an aching pain in his low back, hips, and buttocks. It was intense enough that he dropped his supplies. His pain amplified when he bent over, picked up the load, and pivoted. Though he had a history of sharp pain in his low back, this was different and accompanied by a weak feeling. He couldn't enjoy playing football, which was depressing. The pain was worsened by lifting, sitting for a long time, or jogging. Twisting was problematic. Walking was fine. He reported that the pain was sometimes incapacitating. When the pain was at its worst, he curled into a fetal position to try to alleviate it.

He sought relief through massage, chiropractic care, and physical therapy. While they briefly helped, the pain returned.

I used several clues to guide me. First, his pain was triggered by lifting a weight and worsened by sitting (Yang Ming). Second, pivoting (Shao Yang) was problematic.

I gave him an acupuncture treatment addressing Yang Ming and Shao Yang and demonstrated the Bamboo Twist (Chapter 13) and Yang Ming's Agony and Surrender (Chapter 31). The patient was able to do both positions lying down without pain. I recommended he practice once a day.

Within a week, he let me know he was doing better and would return when he needed help. In two months, he came back for an office visit and reported he was feeling much better. The pain was sometimes completely gone. He returned to jogging with minimal soreness and weakness but no pain, which, by his account, was a big improvement. He sometimes felt discomfort in his low back and sacrum, and that's what we addressed next by working on the Tai Yang level. I recommended he add Locust Looks East and West (Chapter 20) and to lessen the frequency of dao yin practice to three times a week.

After two years, this patient continues to be able to do his daily activities for both work and recreation. He reports he hasn't had any significant or lasting pain. He received only two acupuncture treatments for his entire course of treatment and continues to do one of the exercises a couple of times a week.

≈

As you can see from these two case studies, it is common to find at least two sinew channels involved in pain or dysfunction. I tell my patients this is because the body is not a collection of separate parts but an intimately integrated system. One channel will come to the rescue of another or share the burden. If we look only at where a problem is showing up—for example, the low back—we might miss the other channels involved as evidenced by the types of movements that make the pain worse. In the first case, we see how working with just one of the affected channels can be sufficient. The second case demonstrates how addressing more than one channel can affect a singular location or zone—in this case, the low back and hips.

CASE 3

My final case is about a participant in one of my community-service dao yin classes at one of our local libraries. Here we see how empowering the practice can be—opening up possibilities and awakening awareness of our healing potential.

Toward the end of this class, we were practicing a couple of dao yin movements for the digestive system. I noticed one of the participants was wiping tears from her face and blowing her nose. It was clear she was having an emotional release. This is not unusual. When we began class, I had reminded the entire group that movement can provoke surfacing emotions. I had invited them, if it felt okay, to stay with the practice as best they could, even as emotions expressed themselves. I had mentioned we were all in the same boat. If someone needed to leave the room because of intense feelings, I had encouraged them to return as soon as they felt ready. A box of tissues was always within reach.

Despite the tears, she stayed until class ended. After the room cleared, she approached me. She shared that earlier in the week she had been called by her medical doctor's office about a recent lab report. Over the phone, she was told there was concern she could have cancer in her digestive tract. The unexpected news was frightening and grief-provoking, as one of her parents had died from this cancer. She told me she was crying because not only had the practice let her get in touch with her emotions from the alarming news, but it had also helped her realize there were things she could do to secure her wellbeing and improve her health. She felt relief to be reminded she had resources and support to address her health concern.

Ouroborus: The Dragon Swallows Its Own Tail

Though we've come to the conclusion of this exploration of dao yin, I hope you, too, feel as if you now have another set of resources to support your continued growth and wellbeing. Whatever sensations, thoughts, emotions, or revelations you encounter, I invite you to meet them with curiosity and compassion. Take heart in whatever emerges. No matter what comes up, the good, the bad, and the beautiful, I trust it can serve a guide.

I like to end my practice with two questions I learned from my friend Nick Pole (2017), author of *Words that Touch, How to Ask Questions Your Body Can Answer*:

- And what do I know now about all that?

- And what difference does knowing that make?

Figures

BASIC POSES

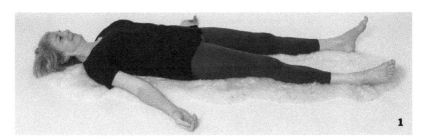

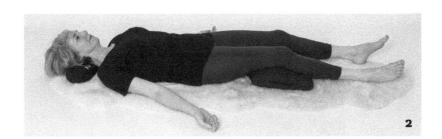

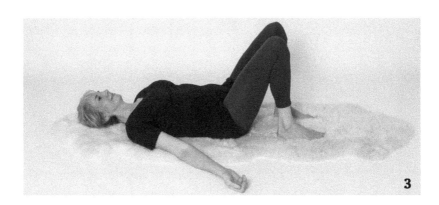

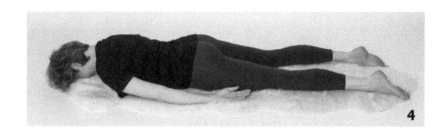

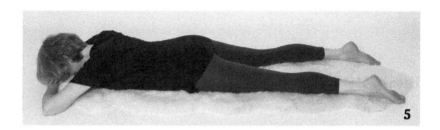

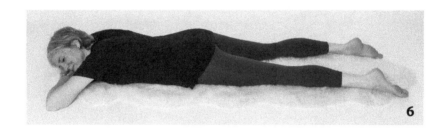

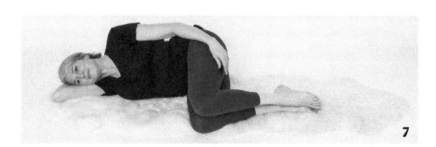

81 AND 81 BELLY RUB

SWIMMING SNAKE

PREPARING TO STAND

LIZARD RUNS ACROSS THE WATER

FROG SHIMMY

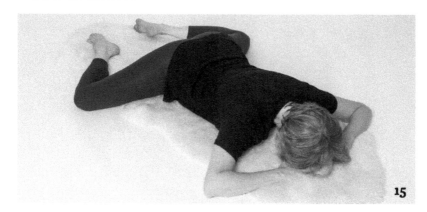

BAMBOO TWIST

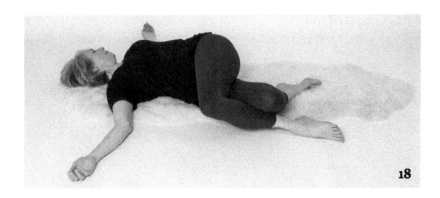

FREE ME

HEAD ROLL AND RELEASE

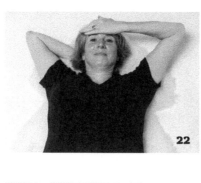

OPENING THE DOORWAYS TO THE EARTH

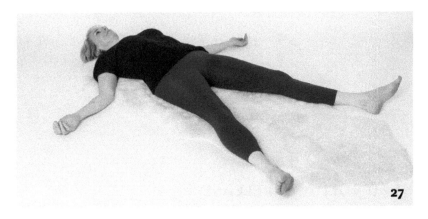

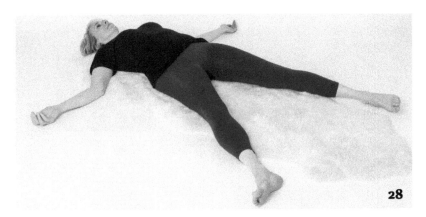

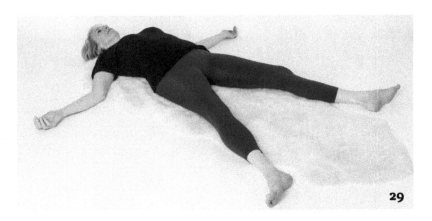

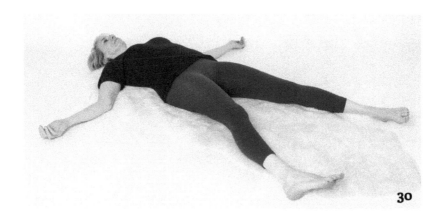

OPENING THE WINDOWS OF HEAVEN

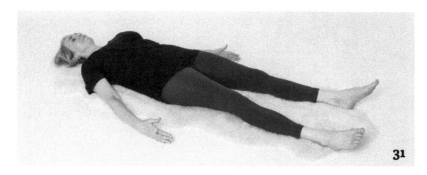

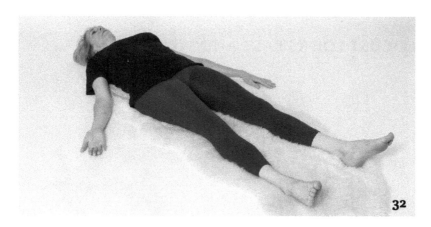

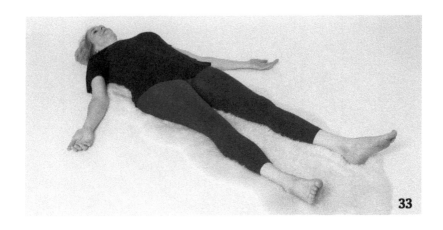

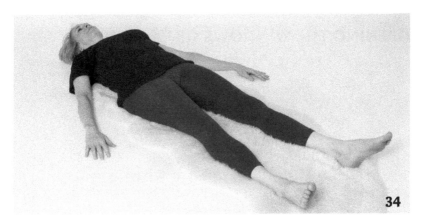

LOCUST LOOKS EAST AND WEST

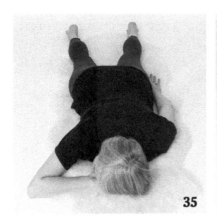

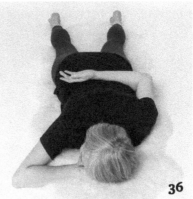

PANNING FOR GOLD

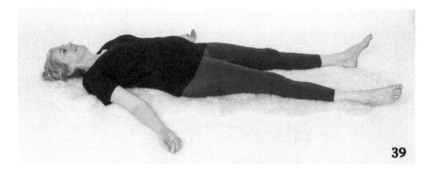

WELCOME BREATH

41

42

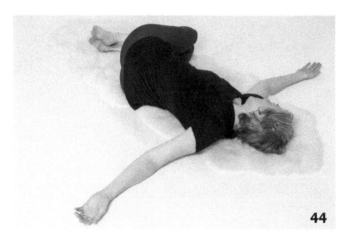

LOCUST LOOKS AHEAD

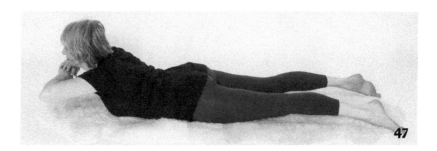

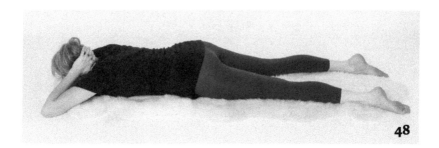

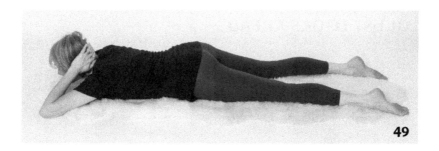

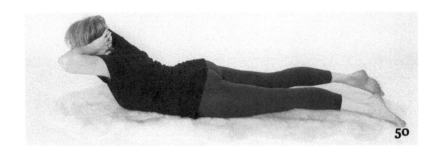

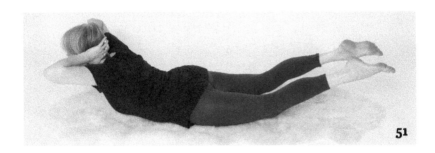

RETURNING TO THE CORE

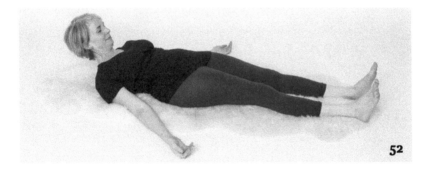

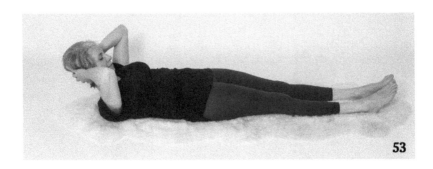

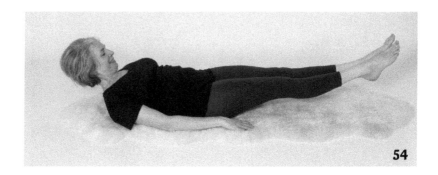

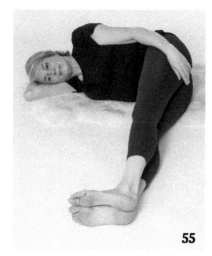

STRETCH THE BOW

FIRE AND WATER

AGONY AND SURRENDER

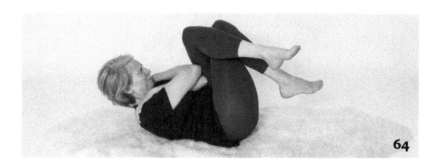

SIDEWINDER

66

67

68

69

70

Illustrations

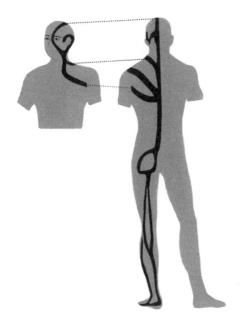

Illustration 1: Tai Yang Urinary Bladder

Illustration 2: Tai Yang Small Intestine

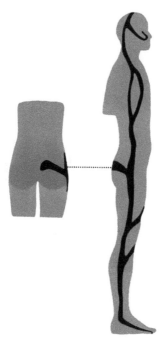

Illustration 3: Shao Yang Gall Bladder

Illustration 4: Shao Yang Triple Heater

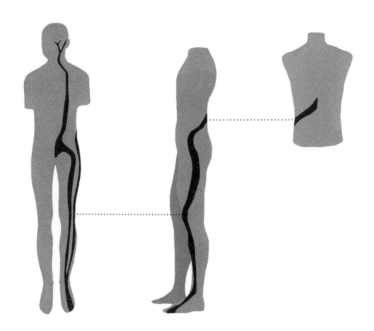

Illustration 5: Yang Ming Stomach

Illustration 6: Yang Ming Large Intestine

Yamas and Niyamas of Yoga

There are two main references I draw from for my understanding of Patanjali's *Yoga Sutras*, a complete text on the philosophy and practice of yoga:

- *Practical Yoga, Ancient and Modern* by Ernest E. Wood

- *The Practice of the Yoga Sutra, Sadhana Pada* by Pandit Rajmani Tigunait, PhD

Please see "Further Reading and Research" at the end of the book for full references.

The five yamas, known as the five abstinences, are self-regulating behaviors involving our interactions with other people and the world at large. Through clear boundaries and conscious action, we can build our magnetism, attracting things that will help us fulfill our life's mission and purpose.

- Ahimsa: do not injure yourself or others.

- Satya: do not lie.

- Asteya: do not steal.

- Brahmacharya: avoid excess or overindulgence.

- Aparigraha: do not be greedy and possessive.

The five niyamas are five daily observances or personal practices that relate to our inner world. These devotions help us direct our energy to love more deeply, inclusively, and unconditionally, with compassion and humility.

- Saucha: be pure of thought, action, and communication.

- Santosha: be content with what we currently have.

- Tapas: practice self-discipline, training your senses through body conditioning and asana (yoga postures), pranayama (breathing practices), pratyhara (sensory withdrawal), and dharana (concentration).

- Svadhyaya: practice self-reflection, self-study, and inner exploration.

- Ishvara Pranidhana: be attentive (to God).

Further Reading and Research

Allen, S. (1997) *The Way of Water and Sprouts of Virtue*. Albany: State University of New York Press.

Arthur, S. (2013) *Early Daoist Dietary Practices: Examining Ways to Health and Longevity*. Lanham: Lexington Books.

Chia, M. (2005) *Energy Balance through the Tao: Exercises for Cultivating Yin Energy*. Rochester: Destiny Books.

Dana, D. (2020) *Polyvagal Exercises for Safety and Connection: 50 Client-Centered Practices*. New York: W.W. Norton & Company.

Dass, R. (1971) *Be Here Now*. San Cristobal: Lama Foundation.

Emoto, M. (2005) *The Secret Life of Water*. Hillsboro: Beyond Words Publishing.

Feng, G. and English, J. (1972) *Lao Tsu: Tao Te Ching*. New York: Vintage Books.

Frawley, D. (2000) *Vedantic Meditation: Lighting the Flame of Awareness*. Berkeley: North Atlantic Books.

Goleman, D. and Davidson, R. (2017) *Altered Traits: Science Reveals How Meditation Changes Your Mind, Brain, and Body*. New York: Penguin Books.

Ho, M.-W. (2008) *The Rainbow and the Worm: The Physics of Organisms*. Singapore: World Scientific Publishing Co.

Lau, D. C. (1963) *Lao Tzu: Tao Te Ching*. London: Penguin Classics.

Lee, B. (1971) "The Way of the Intercepting Fist." *Longstreet* [TV series], Season 1, Episode 1.

Hinrichs, T. J. and Barnes, L. (2013) *Chinese Medicine and Healing: An Illustrated History*. Cambridge: The Belknap Press of Harvard University Press.

Hinton, D. (2013) *The Four Chinese Classics: Tao Te Ching, Chuang Tzu, Analects, Mencius*. Berkeley: Counterpoint Press.

Hua-Ching, Ni (1998) *Attune Your Body with Dao-In: Taoist Exercise for a Long and Happy Life*. Los Angeles: Tao of Wellness Press.

Klein, J. (1984) *The Ease of Being*. Durham: The Acorn Press.

Kohn, L. (2008) *Chinese Healing Exercises: The Tradition of Dao yin*. Honolulu: University of Hawai'i Press.

Kohn, L. (2012) *A Source Book in Chinese Longevity*. St. Petersburg: Three Pines Press.

Kuriyama, S. (2002) *The Expressiveness of the Body and the Divergence of Greek and Chinese Medicine*. New York: Zone Books.

Muir, J. (1911) *My First Summer in the Sierra*. Boston: Houghton Mifflin.

Pole, N. (2017) *Words that Touch: How to Ask Questions Your Body Can Answer.* London: Singing Dragon.

Rossi, M. (2018) *Listening Like Water: Depth and Connection as Part of the Healing Process.* St. Louis: Qiological Podcast. Accessed on 22/1/2021 at www.qiological.com.

Rossi, M. and Pole, N. (2020) *Dao of Communication.* St. Louis: Qiological Podcast. Accessed on 22/1/2021 at www.qiological.com.

Singh, J. (1991) *The Yoga of Delight, Wonder, and Astonishment: A Translation of the Vijnana-bhairava.* Albany: State University of New York Press.

Snyder, G. (1965) *Riprap and Cold Mountain Poems.* Washington, DC: Shoemaker and Hoard.

Sri Chinmoy (1988) *Beyond Within.* New York: Agni Press.

Sri Marharshi (ed.) (1996) *Words of Grace.* Tamilnadu: V.S. Ramanan.

Tigunait, P. R. (2017) *The Practice of the Yoga Sutra, Sadhana Pada.* Honesdale: Himalayan International Institute of Yoga Science and Philosophy of the U.S.A.

Van der Kolk, B. (2014) *The Body Keeps the Score: Brain, Mind, and Body in the Healing of Trauma.* New York. Penguin Books.

Wilms, S. (2014) *Twelve Characters: A Transmission of Wang Fengyi's Teachings.* Corbett: Happy Goat Productions.

Wolff, R. (2001) *Original Wisdom: Stories of an Ancient Way of Knowing.* Rochester: Inner Traditions International.

Wood, E. (1948) *Practical Yoga, Ancient and Modern.* New York: E.P. Dutton & Co. Inc.

Yang, D. (2018) *Prescribing 'Guiding and Pulling': The Institutionalisation of Therapeutic Exercise in Sui China (581–618).* Doctoral thesis (PhD). London: University College London.

Index

81 and 81 Belly Rub 34–5

abdominal massage 34–5
abdominal muscles 110, 132
abstinences 87–90, 211
acceptance, self- 103–4
acupuncture points 77–80, 153, 172
aging 102
Agony and Surrender 132–5, 184
Ah-Ma-Ohm 129–31
anxiety 180
assessment
    mobility 176–7
    sitting/lifting pain 178, 184
    twisting 177–8
attachments 124, 132
attention
    expansion of 70–1
    relating attributes of water to 17
    to feelings in body 24
awakening 71
awareness
    coming back to 169
    as empty place 40–1

Bamboo Twist 61–3, 178, 184
barre prop 38
beginner's mind 37, 39–42, 41
belly rub 34–5
blood circulation 77
body and breath scan 31–3, 164–5

body language 70
bowel movement support 34
breath and body scan 31–3, 164–5
breathwork
    breathing technique 166
    Panning for Gold: Activating
        the Diaphragm 95–7
    Welcome Breath 98–102, 178
Bright Yang channels 178

case studies
    Agony and Surrender 184
    Bamboo Twist 184
    emotional release 185
    Locust Looks East and
        West 182–3, 184
change (water cycle as) 17–8
channels 172–8
chaos (traffic) 48–9, 51–2
"Chinese Farmer Story" 59
Chinese medicine train-
       ing 116–7, 144–7
Chinmoy, Sri 20
Circulate and Harmonize
    Self-Massage 148–53
collective mindset 51–2
commandments of yoga 87–90, 211–2
confidence 36
contentment (cultivating) 87–90
curiosity 168–9
cycling 48–9, 51

Damon, Betsy 136–9
Dao De Jing 159
dao yin practice
    meaning of dao yin 19
    moderation in 163, 179
    movement in 162
    observing effects of 163–6
    overview 157–60
    repetition 167
    significance of lying down 160–2
    speed 166–7
    tension and holding 163
    timing 167–8, 179
Daoism
    philosophy of 158–9
    reverence for water 17
death 116, 126–8
decision-making 177
detoxification 138–9
disappointment/discouragement 178
dissociation 23
doing (letting go of) 41

ego 36, 37–9
81 and 81 Belly Rub 34–5
emotional release 20, 22, 185
Emoto, Masaru 103
energy, stuck 50–2
environmental triggers 172
ethical living 88–90
eyes (potency of) 167

Fire and Water 121–3
food triggers 172
forgiveness (of self) 88
Frawley, David 39
Free Me 64–7
Frisky (cat) 125–8
Frog Shimmy 56–7, 178

gall bladder 95, 174, 177
Greater Yang channels 176
grief 124–5
grounding
    81 and 81 Belly Rub 34–5
    Free Me exercise 64–7
    Opening the Doorways to
        the Earth 77–80
    yoga and 23
Guan Yin 49–51

habitual patterns 24, 162
harvesting herbs 145–6
Head Roll and Release 73–6
healing elixir 49–51
heart 95, 117, 121–3
Heraclitus 37
herbal medicine 145–7
hips (opening) 56–7
Hollis, Joe 144–7
homeostasis 177
horseback riding 68–72
humour 39

insecurity 103–4
integrated systems 184–5
intention 25

jaw tension 73
journaling 180

Kaptchuk, Ted 116
Keepers of the Water 136
kidneys 117, 121
Klein, Jean 39–41
knee pain 77

Lao Zi 26
large intestine 175, 178
Lesser Yang channels 177–8
letting go 132
liver 95
Living Water Garden 136–9
Lizard Runs Across the
    Water 53–5, 176
Locust Looks Ahead 105–9, 177
Locust Looks East and West
    91–4, 176, 182–3, 184
love (attraction to romantic) 85–90
lungs 95
lying down (significance of) 160–2

massage, self- 148–53
mental-emotional well-
    being 81–4, 180
meridians 172
metaphors
    dao yin 158–60
    water 17, 58
mindful movement 24, 68–72

moderation (in practice) 163, 179
Muir, John 115–6
musculoskeletal system
    balance 77–80

neck tension 73
niyamas 87–90, 211–2
non-judgment 41
numbness 91

observances 87–90, 211–2
obstacle (illusion of) 58–60
Opening the Doorways to
    the Earth 77–80
Opening the Windows
    of Heaven 81–4
organization skills 177

pancreas 95
Panning for Gold 95–7
paralysis 91
pelvic conditions 61
planning skills 177
Pole, Nick 186
posture improvement 53–5
Preparing to Stand 46–7
present moment awareness 42–3
prone pose 28–9
purification 138–9
purity of water 85–90

qigong training 49–52

regret 124–5
reishi mushrooms 145
repetition 167
respiratory tract infections 98
Returning to the Core 110–4
righteousness 59–60
romantic love (attraction to) 85–90

safe container 42
scan (body and breath) 31–3, 164–5
self-acceptance 103–4
self-awareness 165
self-diagnosis 171–80
self-doubt 103–4
self-empowerment 19

self-knowledge 159
self-massage (Circulate and
    Harmonize) 148–53
self-reflection 88, 165
self-transformation 138–9
sensitivity 168–9
sensory organs
    issues with 91
    opening 73, 81–4
sequencing 168
Shan, Han 16
Shan Ren Dao 88–90
Shao Yang channels 177–8
Shao Yang Gall Bladder 95, 174, 177
Shao Yang Triple Heater 174, 177
shoulders
    opening 56–7
    tension in 73
side-lying pose 29–30
Sidewinder 140–3, 178
silence (being comfortable with) 24
sinew channels 172–80
small intestine 90, 173, 176
speed (of practice) 166–7
spine
    lengthening 53–5
    stimulating 105
spiraling movement 137–8
spleen 95
spontaneous qigong 49–52
Stand, Preparing to 46–7
stomach 95, 175, 178
Stomach 30 (acupuncture point) 153
"Story of the Chinese Farmer" 59
straps (yoga) 38
stress (as trigger) 172
Stretch the Bow 118–20, 177
stuck emotions 22
stuck energy 50–2
supine pose 27–8
Swimming Snake 43–5, 178

Tai Yang channels 176
Tai Yang Small Intestine 173, 176
Tai Yang Urinary Bladder 173, 176
teeth 105
Ten Commandments of
    yoga 87–90, 211–2
tendinomuscular channels 172–80

tension and holding 163
timing of practice 167–8, 179
toes (pressing) 46
traffic (chaos) 48–9, 51–2
triple heater 174, 177
twists
    as aggravator 177
    Bamboo Twist 61–3, 178, 184
    in life 138–9
    Sidewinder 140–3, 178

uncertainty 21–2, 36
urinary bladder 173, 176

vagus nerve 95
vision
    potency of the eyes 167
    stimulating 105

water
    beginner's mind and 41
    cycle of 124–8
    influences on 103
    Living Water Garden 136–9

as metaphor 17, 58
purity of 85–90
role in community 15
soothing presence of 16, 58
spiraling movement of 137–8
yielding quality of 58–60
waterfalls 58–60
Watts, Alan 59
Way of the Virtuous Person 88–90
weight (bearing too much) 178, 184
Welcome Breath 98–102, 178

yamas 87–90, 211
Yang Ming channels 178
Yang Ming Large Intestine 175, 178
Yang Ming Stomach 175, 178
yielding quality of water 58–60
yoga, first experience of 21–2, 25–6
Yuanfang, Chao 19
Yuen, Jeffrey 18–9

Zhuangzi 40